D1624475

SECRETS OF COACHING CHAMPIONSHIP BASEBALL

796.35
D87

SECRETS OF COACHING CHAMPIONSHIP BASEBALL

KEN DUGAN

PARKER PUBLISHING COMPANY, INC., WEST NYACK, NEW YORK

© 1980, *by*

PARKER PUBLISHING COMPANY, INC.
West Nyack, N.Y.

*All rights reserved. No part of this
book may be reproduced in any form or
by any means, without permission in
writing from the publisher.*

Library of Congress Cataloging in Publication Data

Dugan, Ken.
 Secrets of coaching championship baseball.

 Includes index.
 1. Baseball coaching. 2. School sports. I. Title.
GV875.5.D83   796.357'077   79-25060
ISBN 0-13-797860-X

Printed in the United States of America

DEDICATION

To the 1977 and 1979 David Lipscomb College National Championship Teams
and
All my friends in Belgium who share my great love for baseball.

137216

FOREWORD

In 40 years of baseball coverage, professional and amateur, I have known no man whom I respect more for his knowledge of the game's complexities—and simplicities—than Coach Ken Dugan of David Lipscomb College in Nashville, Tennessee.

Every team he ever coached has enjoyed a winning season. There have been championships almost without number. When you read this latest book of his, you'll understand why.

If reliability and clarity are characteristics of Coach Dugan's writing, a mastery of baseball techniques and the ability to impart that know-how to his teams have been part and parcel of his success. They are among the best prepared—to win—on the collegiate level.

I know that if I were actively associated with the game as a coach or manager, or as a player, I would want this book within easy reach. It is written in language that fans will understand, too, giving it a general appeal.

When Coach Dugan wrote his first book, *How to Organize and Coach Winning Baseball* (1971), I reviewed it for my paper. That superbly organized collection of chapters on how to play, a guide to winning baseball, had several printings. I predict similar popularity for this handbook.

George Leonard
Sports Editor
Nashville Banner

HOW THESE CHAMPIONSHIP COACHING SECRETS WILL HELP YOU

The purpose of this book is to provide championship coaching secrets for individuals interested in advancing their knowledge of the skills and strategies of baseball. Although this comprehensive instructional material has been planned especially for the high school and college level, it meets the needs of the coach of any age group. The aim constantly in mind throughout its preparation has been to help you in developing the abilities of your players and to make you more keenly aware of the most up-to-date thinking concerning the development of baseball skills and game strategies.

The book has been organized and outlined in such a way that you may apply this knowledge to the broad spectrum of baseball skills. The individual who carefully studies this book and supplements it with practice and personal instruction should acquire a thorough understanding of secrets in the techniques of the game. You will understand fully the "why" of skill development in baseball and you will find that the methods and techniques suggested as secrets of the game are based on something more substantial than opinion. It will make you more aware of the personal qualities and insight necessary for success.

By reviewing the materials, you will increase your ability to judge players' skills and your information concerning game strategy. You will find valuable teaching tips, methods for conducting tryouts, the proper way to take infield, strategy aids, and a system for developing a championship team. You will learn the latest techniques in baserunning, the positive approach to bunting, and how to teach young players to throw correctly and to hit the curveball. You will learn the secrets of securing the most efficient results from batting practice, how to keep everyone busy during practice, how to win games on the bench, and why it takes more than nine players to win any baseball game.

The chapter on coaching warrants special attention, since it deals with many of the problems you face. This chapter attempts to achieve some understanding of the educational aspects of baseball. Such topics as The Coach as a Teacher, Organizer, Disciplinarian, Leader in the Community, and Faculty Member are included. Other subjects given attention in this chapter are public relations, players' attitudes, and The Coach as an Actor.

No attempt is made to include all the techniques of baseball; rather, stress is placed on the most successful or secret methods of coaching and playing. An attempt is made to answer questions which have been in the minds of coaches like yourself for a long time. This is a book that can be used in the classroom or on the playing field, solving many problems confronting you.

Some of the little known procedures which will be of special aid to you are a section on batting faults and how to correct them, a section on hitting in the "clutch," a section on batting slumps, and discussions of batters' weaknesses and how to pitch to them, the correct way to initiate a run-down, pick-off plays that will work, and the squeeze play and how to make it effective.

Other distinctive features are the chapters on Championship Offensive and Championship Defensive Play, which discuss team defense, cut-off plays, relays, bunt situations, and defensing the delayed and double steal.

Completing this coaching tool are secret game-winning tips on such topics as selecting the starting lineup, proper techniques in sacrifice bunting, pitching readiness, and teaching the outfielders how to get a jump on fly balls. Other new techniques and methods are noted in discussions of each defensive position and all the fine arts of offense. These features, added to the presentation of the basic principles, make this a complete baseball guidebook for you as a coach.

Ken Dugan

ACKNOWLEDGMENTS

The author would like to acknowledge the many people who have helped make this book possible:

To Dr. Lewis Maiden and Dr. Leota Maiden for their invaluable help in preparing the manuscript;

To Mrs. Mary Carrigan for typing the manuscript;

To President Willard Collins, Vice President Carl McKelvey, and Dean Earl Dennis of David Lipscomb College for their invaluable advice and encouragement;

To the many fine friends and coaches with whom the author has been associated while coaching the game: George Leonard, Sports Editor, *Nashville Banner*, Nashville, Tennessee; Jerry Potter, sports writer, *Clarion Ledger*, Jackson, MS; Jeff Hanna, sports writer, *The Virginia Pilot*, Norfolk, VA; Coach Curtis Putnam, Assistant Baseball Coach, David Lipscomb College; Roy Pardue, Pitching Coach, David Lipscomb College; Gaston Panaye, Jos Lenaerts, Jack Reinenbergh and Gilbert Naessens from Antwerp, Belgium; John Herbold, Lakewood, California; Danny Litwhiler, Michigan State University; Chuck Bafaro, Pacific University; Robert E. Smith, Greenville, IL; Robert Starcher, Malone College; Charles Sarver, Biola College; Dave Brazell, Grand Canyon College.

The contents of this book include many ideas of these people and others with whom the author has been associated while playing and coaching.

CONTENTS

1

SECRETS OF ACCELERATED BATTING PRACTICE AND TEAM ORGANIZATION

Baseball players like to play for a coach whose program is well organized, who knows the game, and who deals with each one of them honestly and fairly. Favoritism and discrimination are absolutely forbidden to the good coach. Each individual on the team should feel he is important to its overall success. Your job is to sell each player on his own ability as well as on the worthiness of the system of play.

You should insist on neatness off the field and absolutely demand it on the field, where it involves sanitation, protection, and good common sense. The appearance of a team can help its performance. All players should wear their uniforms in the same manner.

THE CAPTAIN

The captain is elected by his teammates or appointed by you. He is a leader among them both on and off the playing field. He always wants to win but never loses his temper in defeat. His sportsmanship should be an inspiration to his teammates.

The captain should communicate with you concerning team problems or individual problems which may be of importance to you. Encourage the captain to express his own feelings, realizing that you have to make all final decisions. An excellent captain can be of great service to the team and the coach.

THE SCHEDULE

When making out a baseball schedule, consider how much money you have to spend on the road trips and how much class time will be missed. The scholastic ability of the players will determine how many classes can be missed. Naturally, you should never jeopardize the scholarship of the players by playing too many games.

If the team is made up of players with little experience, the easiest games should be the first on the schedule. Early victories give the players confidence and add to team morale. You will have a better opportunity to develop the squad if there is a big margin of victories early in the season.

Another factor in scheduling that must be considered is the number of pitchers on the squad. One secret to winning a large number of games is to have the right pitcher rested before the important games. The easy games will usually take care of themselves if the team has the proper mental approach to each game.

CONDUCTING TRYOUTS

Each year, new prospects will be coming out for the team. At Lipscomb, "tryouts" are conducted during the fall baseball program. During this time, each new prospect will have a better opportunity to display his skills. There is no pressure to prepare for scheduled games, and the weather usually is ideal at this time of year. Many prospects have played ball all summer, and they are in excellent physical condition for performance on the field. The fall practice may last several weeks, with games being played every Friday and Saturday. When fall practice has concluded, the coach has chosen his squad and a smaller group to work with the following spring. This is also an excellent time for returning lettermen to work on their weaknesses. If the facilities are available, the fall baseball program is recommended. The fall program can be the secret to championship play the following spring.

Although the selection of players is mostly subjective judgment on the part of the coach, he should be impartial and deliberate in making decisions. He should develop a checklist that will help him in his selections. It is very difficult to remember names and abilities when several people are trying out. When you are picking the team, both the offensive and defensive abilities of each player must be considered. For example, a good hitter may be a weak defensive player and of less value to the team than another player who does not hit as well but plays much stronger defense. It should also be mentioned that some players are routine in practice but outstanding in game situations. For this reason, practice games are recommended. Another factor a coach should consider in selecting his team is the player's attitude toward his school work. A player with low grades is likely to be one who will have trouble remaining eligible. Good grades, good study habits, and proper attitude toward school work go hand in hand with the potential athletic ability of the player. It is difficult to discipline one's self in one area and not be the same type of individual in another. The player who is always having trouble in school sooner or later will hurt the team. The best student is usually the best athlete.

The length of "tryouts" will vary with the circumstances, such as the number of coaches, the number of people trying out, the facilities, and the length of practice time. Some coaches use numbers to evaluate the player's skills. Each skill will receive a number ranging from one through ten—the higher the number the greater the skill. The coach must make a complete list of skills to be evaluated that are meaningful to him.

As "tryouts" are being conducted and players rated, the coach should keep the desired qualities for each position in mind. Some players play one position when they would be more effective in another. Each player should be given a chance at his first choice, but the coach should not hesitate to move him to another position if it will help the team.

THE BATTING ORDER

The coach must arrange his batting order according to the offensive ability of each person in the lineup. The secret is to analyze the capabilities of all players and distribute their respective strengths in the batting order so they can make the greatest contribution. In general, a team's best hitter should be at the top of the batting list, to assure him a maximum number of times at bat. The first seven positions should be given considerable thought, with the idea of balancing the lineup so that the attack is as strong as possible from the leadoff man through the ninth hitter.

The first batter should be one with a special talent for getting on base. He should have a keen batting eye and not be tempted to swing at bad pitches. He should be fast of foot and a good base runner. His speed will force the opponents into more errors. He may be an effective bunter and, if so, he will keep the defense on edge. The modern day leadoff man may be a power hitter.

The number-two batter should be a skillful bunter and an excellent hit-and-run man. His primary requisite should be the ability to make contact with the ball. Ideally, he is a left-handed hitter who has bat control. A left-handed hitter in this spot will make it easier for the runner to steal. Speed is desirable to keep down double plays, but it is not as necessary as it is for the first batter.

The number-three batter usually will be the player with the highest batting average on the team. He should be fast on his feet so he will have more opportunities to score on hits by the fourth batter. If the number-three man bats left-handed, the number-four man should hit right-handed.

The fourth batter should be a long-ball hitter who can hit with runners on base. The assumption is that one or two of the first three batters will reach base, and in this spot he will have the opportunity to drive in runs. The number-four batter may be one of the two best hitters on the team.

The fifth batter's qualifications are much the same as those of number four. If a consistent hitter is not available, stress should be placed on the ability to hit the long ball.

The sixth batter should have the same qualifications as the first batter, with the added ability to drive in runs. He will have many opportunities because of the hitting abilities of the third, fourth and fifth batters. A real "clutch" hitter is an ideal player for this position.

The seventh batter has much the same qualifications as the second, with more stress placed on hitting the long ball and driving in runs. Also, the seventh batter could be a slower runner than the second batter.

In amateur ball, where the teams do not play daily, as in high school and college, the pitcher and the catcher may be placed in the batting order according to their hitting ability. Another factor in deciding if the pitcher hits ninth would be if he stays in the game or plays some other position after being removed from the mound. If he is no longer in the lineup, who will replace him in the batting order? This must be considered in determining the lineup in order to have an effective batting order.

THE DEFENSIVE LINEUP

From the defensive standpoint, the strength of a team is first considered down the middle. This would include the pitcher, catcher, shortstop, second baseman and center fielder. Then the first baseman, third baseman, left fielder, and right fielder are chosen.

Many baseball experts say that pitching is as much as 75 per cent of the defensive strength of a team. If this is true, pitching must be given first consideration. In judging a pitcher, the coach must consider control as the most important asset in amateur baseball. A player with a good fastball, mental poise, physical strength, and endurance has all the basic tools for becoming an outstanding pitcher. But in amateur baseball these qualifications are rare. Size is not a factor in viewing prospects, but a player who has a loose throwing motion and can get the ball over the plate has a great chance of being a successful pitcher.

The catcher is second in importance, since he is the field

general. He should be someone who knows baseball, has good hands, and can handle all types of thrown balls. A man who has a strong throwing arm, is alert to the game situations, and is an aggressive leader is the ideal type to work behind the plate. Good size and speed are assets but not essentials.

Defensively, the second baseman has more responsibility than any other infielder, and he must be the second best fielder of ground balls on the team. Speed, quickness, and mental alertness are essential to his play. A strong throwing arm is a desired asset, since he will make many throws to first base from the second-base area.

The shortstop should have a strong throwing arm and be the best all-around fielder of ground balls on the team. He should have excellent speed and the ability to cover a great deal of ground.

The center fielder's requirements are superior speed, a strong throwing arm, and the ability to cover a lot of ground. He should be adept at judging fly balls and charging ground balls hit in his area.

The first baseman should have quick hands and be able to handle all types of throws in his direction. He does not have to be exceptionally fast, and his throwing arm is not as important as that of the other infielders; but he should be able to field ground balls and shift his feet at first base.

The third baseman must have a good pair of hands with quick reflexes and an accurate, reasonably strong throwing arm. He must be able to field slow-hit balls quickly and block hard-hit ground balls.

The right fielder should have a strong throwing arm and be a good judge of fly balls. Speed is desirable but not as essential as in center field.

The left fielder may have the weakest arm of the three outfielders, but speed and fielding ability are of great importance. The left fielder usually will have many fielding opportunities in amateur baseball.

PRACTICE ROUTINE

One of the primary duties of a baseball coach is to keep his players busy every minute of a practice session in order to impress upon them that they must work to improve themselves. Practice with half the team merely standing around cannot be tolerated. Practice that is organized, with everyone busy and some teaching taking place, is ideal.

The team should set a definite practice time when everyone will be on the field. This helps in organizing the practice. If some players can come to the field earlier, they should be encouraged to do so, since provision can be made for them to work on weaknesses.

The first responsibility of the players when they arrive on the field is to get themselves loose—their legs as well as their arms. The major part of any workout centers in batting practice. It is here that a coach can get the most from his time if he has activities organized.

BATTING PRACTICE

It is important for each player to take as many swings as possible during this period of time. Players, pitchers, or coaches with good control should pitch batting practice when the hitters are working on timing. However, on the last round it is advisable for someone to throw three-quarter speed and curveballs with no attempt to fool the batter. This increases his chances of hitting the ball and develops confidence. As practice progresses toward the opening game, the hitter should see more curveballs each day.

Every team should have a policy concerning the number of balls bunted or the number of swings taken, so that all players have the same amount of practice. Some teams favor a certain number of swings, even though the ball is fouled or missed. By this procedure, the hitter is more likely to swing at good pitches and thus increase the number of rounds of batting practice.

When the batter takes his last swing on each round, he runs to first base. Early in pre-season workouts, he should run straight through the base, concentrating on getting out of the batter's box. As the season approaches, he should make his turn at first base. Then as the pitcher takes his stretch and the next batter is bunting, the former hitter is working on getting his lead and jump on the pitcher to steal second.

A popular drill in batting practice is to play "base hit" between the infielders and the outfielders. Each group is allowed ten swings, if enough time remains in batting practice, and the group with the most total hits is the winner. The coach can reward the winners with additional swings or make the losers do additional running. The pitchers are used to shag in the outfield.

For a fast-moving batting practice, several baseballs are desirable so that the pitcher need not wait for the balls to return to him. Two ball bags should be used, one filled with balls on the mound for the pitcher and one for a shagger on the edge of the grass behind second base (Diag. 1-1). The shagger is placed in this position to avoid the danger of his being hit by a batted ball. This also eliminates the problem of balls being thrown on the mound or infield. All players are instructed to return batted balls to the shagger, and they should be thrown on the ground to him, not in the air. This usually is a good job for a pitcher, since it requires a great deal of bending. When the shagger begins to fill his bag with baseballs, he takes them to the mound between hitters, so batting practice pitchers will always have plenty of balls on hand. This system keeps batting practice moving and places the shagger in a relatively safe place.

It is a general rule to hit ground balls to the infielders during batting practice. The fungo hitters who have this duty should stand near the batting cage, but out of range of a batted ball (Diag. 1-1). The fungo hitters should refrain from hitting the ball until the batter has hit the pitch, or the ball has passed the plate. This prevents injuries to infielders. In pre-season workouts, each infielder should receive at least a hundred ground balls each day. If the first baseman has a protective wire screen, the infielders can throw to first base. Batting practice is also an excellent time for the infielders to work on the double play.

While the infielders are receiving their ground balls and taking batting practice, someone should hit fly balls to the outfielders. A few of the outfielders may be taking batting practice, while the others are fielding fly balls. It usually is best for the outfielders to line up and then have balls hit to their left and right. After a few practice sessions, they should have balls hit over their heads and in front of them.

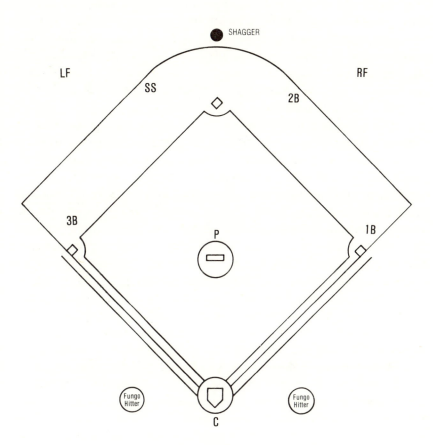

Diagram 1-1

If a player is not receiving fungos during batting practice, he should assume a fielding position and play the ball off the bat as he would in a game. One ball hit to a fielder off the bat in batting practice is worth ten balls hit off a fungo.

Game situations can be stressed during batting practice by placing runners on the bases and giving them certain directions. The runner then must react to where the ball is hit off the bat during batting practice. This works well with runners on second and third base concerning the decisions they must make in tagging up on fly balls and advancing on ground balls.

Many mechanical devices are available to facilitate batting practice, such as the batting tee, pitching machine, iso-swing, and protective screens for the pitcher.

The batting tee is beneficial in pre-season workouts if a player is having trouble with the angle of a swing in relation to the height of a pitch and the position of the ball over the plate. A tee can also help to improve coordination of the stride and swing during a batting slump.

The pitching machine has merit, even though it does not simulate the action of a pitcher. In pre-season workouts, the hitter needs to take as many swings as possible, and the machine can fill a need when no one who can get the ball over the plate is available. Lipscomb has a commercially built machine placed inside an enclosed area where all hitters work on the straight, medium-speed pitches. After a round of thirty swings, the hitter moves to the diamond, where a pitcher is ready to throw curves and fastballs. This practice is beneficial to the pitcher as well as the hitter. By using the pitching machine, members of the team are able to take sixty swings almost every day and still have time for the other aspects of practice. The machine can be valuable in teaching the mechanics of bunting, wherein the bunting practice can be divorced from batting.

A protective screen for the pitcher during batting practice is beneficial since he is less than sixty feet from the plate when the batter hits the ball. A screen about five feet high, placed a proper distance in front of the pitching mound so it does not worry the pitcher when he is throwing, is advisable so that he can be fully protected after delivering the pitch.

GAME PREPARATIONS

The coach should complete game plans several days in advance. The practice sessions should be tailored to fit the opposition. If the coach knows that the opponents will use a left-handed pitcher, his batting practice should be against left-handed throwing. If he thinks the opposing team may use a curveball pitcher, batting practice should be against someone throwing curves. Careful analysis and planning can win ball games before the players take the field.

It is sound procedure to discuss the known strength and weakness of the opposition with all team members present. Discuss the hitting abilities, the speed of the players, the throwing abilities of the outfielders, and any other points that may have a bearing on the game.

The coach should instruct the pitchers who may be used to take a thorough workout two days before the game. The day before the game, they should throw very little, and the workout should be easy. General practice the day before the game should be cut short, under normal conditions. Usually, one hour and thirty minutes is ample time. If the team has been losing, or bad weather has limited the practice time, the coach may want to work out longer.

PRE-GAME BATTING PRACTICE

In pre-game batting practice, the infielders should receive several ground balls off a fungo bat, and the outfielders should play the balls from the bat. Then during infield practice, the outfielders will receive their fungos. If the team is playing on an unfamiliar field, this procedure will give them an opportunity to adjust to the surroundings.

At the end of pre-game batting practice, most teams will bring the starters in to take some extra swings. They usually are allowed one swing each until the time runs out. During this period a little spirit and life should get into the squad. The players who are not starting should spread over the outfield to chase the balls.

All batting practice is intended primarily for the benefit of the hitter, especially during pre-game hitting. This does not indicate that slow pitches should be thrown to the batter. This type of batting practice does more harm than good. The batter needs to see some three-quarter speed pitches, along with curveballs. There should be no attempt to fool the batter. Some coaches like the pitchers to throw full speed when the hitters are called in at the end of pre-game batting practice. Other coaches like straight three-quarter-speed pitches to be thrown, so the hitter can develop his confidence.

While batting practice is in progress, the coach should be on the field, reminding players of special instructions. He should call attention to the wind, the sun, and any peculiarities of the playing area. He should instruct the pitcher concerning the amount of time to warm up according to the weather conditions. The outfielders should be reminded of the effects of wind conditions on fly balls. The coach should verify all arrangements with outfield fungo hitters, relay men, and fungo fielders. Additional infielders who are to take part in the infield workout should be notified. Any other advice that will help win the game should be exploited by the coach. Batting practice can be boring or interesting, depending on what is done and the organization the coach has placed on this period of time. Baseball games are won or lost during practice sessions.

During the opposition's batting practice session, the coach and his entire squad should observe the hitters. Possible batting weaknesses that are detected should be discussed by coach, pitcher, and catcher. The infielders and outfielders should be making mental notes on who pulls the ball or hits late.

Infielders and outfielders should warm up again for a few minutes before infield practice by throwing.

OUTFIELD-INFIELD ROUTINE

Fielding practice is an important part of baseball. It is important that a team get the most from this type of drill. For this to be done, each player must be warmed up adequately, so that he can throw hard without hurting his arm. Also, such a practice routine must be organized to present game-like situations.

Usually, two or three ground balls are hit to each outfielder at the start of the practice, so that throws may be made to second and third base and to the plate. The infielders cover bases and take their various cut-off positions on such throws to practice the duties they are expected to perform in the game.

The coach generally hits to the outfield from a point near the pitcher's mound for throws by the outfielders, and he may hit infield practice from either side of the plate. Fungos to the outfielders are usually hit before infield practice, and during infield practice the outfielders take additional fly balls. These fungos are hit from a spot on the outfield side of the infield to avoid striking anyone.

The outfielders' routine of throwing to the various bases consists of three rounds of two throws each. The routine consists of the following:

Round 1

    1. IF to 2B (hit ball near left-field line)

    2. CF to 2B (hit ball to left of center field)

    3. RF to 2B (hit ball near right field line)

Round 2

    1. LF to 3B (hit ball to left-center field)

    2. CF to 3B (hit ball straight to center field)

    3. RF to 3B (hit ball straight to right field)

Round 3

    1. LF to C (hit ball to left field)

    2. CF to C (hit ball to center field)

    3. RF to C (hit ball to right field)

A common infield routine consists of approximately six rounds during which each infielder and the catcher fields a ball to complete one round. The number may be increased to seven or eight rounds. Prior to the first round, a good procedure is to have the infield in, with the throw going to the plate, and the ball being hit at each infielder. This routine works on cutting the runner down at the plate. At the end of practice, each infielder fields a slowly hit ball and throws to first base. On these two routines the catcher does not throw to the bases.

The following six rounds are standard procedures for infield practice, in which the ball is hit to the first player listed and then thrown around the infield as indicated by the bases or plate:

Round 1 (to first base; ball hit directly at each man)

    1. 3B-1B-C-3B-2B-1B-C

    2. SS-1B-C-SS-3B-C

    3. 2B-1B-C-2B-3B-C

    4. 1B-SS-1B-C

    5. C-1B-SS-C

Round 2

    Same as first round, except hit the ball to infielder's left.

Round 3 (double play; ball hit to infielder's left)

    1. 3B-2B-1B-C-3B-C

    2. SS-2B-1B-C-SS-C

    3. 2B-SS-1B-C-2B-C

    4. 1B-SS-1B-C

    5. C-SS-1B-C

Round 4

    Same as third round, except hit the ball to infielder's right.

Round 5 (to first base; ball hit to infielder's right)

    Same as Rounds 1 and 2

Round 6

    The ball is hit slowly to each infielder, and the throw is made to first base as he charges in. The infielder continues off the field to complete infield practice.

In order to complete the above fielding routine in ten minutes, which is usually allotted for pre-game infield and outfield practice, the coach uses at least three baseballs. This allows for balls getting by the defense. The coach should try to keep two balls in play, hitting a second ball just as the ball previously hit completes a cycle.

CONDITIONING

The majority of today's baseball players are not well-conditioned athletes. There appears to be a prevailing attitude among ball players that they can attain a satisfactory state of physical condition simply by playing the game. Studies at Lipscomb prove that players cannot play themselves into top physical condition because of the limited physical demands of the game itself.

On most teams the only players in top physical condition are the pitchers, and the coaches usually "run" them into condition. Many players with talent never reach their potential because of poor physical conditioning. Too many players do not hustle on the ground ball back to the pitcher or take the extra base during the second game of a doubleheader.

The aura which surrounds the championship team is the desire of each player to hustle on every play. Only the great athletes hustle every day on every play. Since most athletes are lazy, they do only as much as the coach requires them to do.

The championship athlete conditions year-round. He realizes that year-round conditioning is important if he wants to stay at the top.

WEIGHT TRAINING

It is in this area of training and conditioning that most baseball players lag behind athletes in other sports. The muscle-boundness myth has prevailed in baseball probably more than in any other sport. There is a widely accepted theory that a baseball player who touches a barbell will become so tight in the shoulders that he will lose the coordination required to perform the baseball skills of hitting and throwing. Studies at Lipscomb have proven this theory to be false. If two players have the same degree of skill in baseball, the stronger one will have a better chance to succeed. Experiments at Lipscomb over the years have shown a very high correlation between strength and success.

Baseball capitalizes on sudden bursts of strength and power but, by its nature, does little to develop them. Hitting, running, and throwing involve the vigorous action of many muscles. Running calls for quick bursts of speed. Hitting and throwing usually involve sudden and vigorous muscular contractions. The body must be properly conditioned for strength and endurance to avoid muscle strain and joint damage. This conditioning can best be accomplished through a program combining weight training, drills, and running.

The winter months provide the dedicated player with an opportunity to strengthen his body. Although the seat of the weakness will vary with the individual, there is one area in which most of today's athletes have the greatest need for development. Tests show that American boys are lacking in upper body strength. This fact should be of great concern to coaches, since almost every baseball skill is performed to some extent with the muscles of the upper body.

The muscles of the shoulders (deltoid, pectoralis major) are probably the most important in hitting a ball with power. These muscles generate the initial force which gets the bat under way and gives the smaller muscles of the arms and hands the strong foundation they need to have maximum contraction. The elbow extensors (triceps) continue the bat along its path, and the muscles of the forearms and hands provide the final impetus. It is important that the wrists be developed to such a degree that they can not only control the direction of the swing but deliver the final blow with maximum power.

THE BENCH

Many coaches overlook the bench as a factor in building a championship team. So much concentration is devoted to fielding nine men that the bench is often neglected. If good discipline and team morale are to be achieved, these players must feel they are members of the squad. In many instances, the reserve players are as valuable as some of the men on the playing field. Baseball is a team game, and this means every man in uniform. Everyone on the squad, when not on the field, should be seated on the bench and should be a participant in the ball game at all times—mentally and emotionally.

An alert bench reflects championship coaching, the kind that insists on attention to detail and instills in every squad member the belief that he is an integral part of a successful organization. He may uncover valuable information about the opponents that will help his team. The bench at Lipscomb on numerous occasions has detected the opponent's signals, pitching faults, and failure to tag bases.

The bench can lend vocal encouragement to the men on the field and help them when possible by shouting instructions to a player pursuing a fly ball nearby. The players on the bench can help the catcher when a runner is stealing by shouting, "There he goes." In addition, they may keep charts, records, and notes which can be very valuable to the coach. Above all, the players on the bench should gear themselves for the time they may actually take part in the game.

CHARTS AND NOTES

A coach, unless he has an exceptional memory, can help himself considerably by keeping charts, records, and notes on his own personnel and on the opposition. Some of the observations will have to be made and recorded during the game or practice sessions. Others are recorded after the day's work or before practice the next day. Over a period of many years, the author has learned it is better not to "trust to memory what can be written down."

During the game, the coach should have a clipboard handy to record observations he makes concerning what is happening on the field. These notes should be thoroughly analyzed before they are discussed with the players. Such observations are the mark of a championship team. How many times has a coach thought of something he should cover in practice and then forgotten it, only to have this omission cost him a game a few weeks later! Sometimes seemingly minor notations prove to be very important. Notes will not necessarily win ball games, but they do help the coach to work toward better organization, which is one of the secrets of championship play.

The author has found that notes taken during the off season are very helpful the next spring. Thoughts that occur during reading or discussing baseball with other coaches are safer written down than left to memory for the next season.

2

COACHING CHAMPIONSHIP HITTING

A great deal of evidence supports the idea that hitting involves the most difficult and complex set of skills in the entire realm of sports. To hit a baseball out of the reach of fielders is a difficult task. Therefore, it is very important that youngsters learn the proper skills correctly. Unsound skill habits are difficult to correct later in life.

Hitting is a natural skill that can be improved with intelligent analysis and diligent practice. Since hitting is such a difficult skill, it requires constant practice by an individual. The athlete must be prepared to devote many extra hours to hitting in order to develop a high level of competence.

The superior hitter is always observing the situation. He looks for tip-offs, the actual pitching move, the pitching pattern, and, particularly, the hurler's most effective pitch. The catcher will call for this pitch more frequently against the good hitters and when men are in scoring position. Although the outstanding hitter will not do much guessing, he will anticipate in certain situations. At Lipscomb it is called the "educated guess." Any time the count is two balls and no strikes, or three balls and one strike, the hitter should look for a certain pitch in a certain part of the strike zone. The championship hitter in this situation will always look for a pitch in the "happy zone." The happy zone is that part of the strike zone where the batter makes the best contact. If the hitter does not get the pitch he is looking for, he takes it. The outstanding hitters usually anticipate more than the poor hitters.

The secret to coaching championship hitting is to teach the players to think aggressively and to develop the patience to wait for the good pitch. The important issue for you is how to teach the players to become more aggressive without their turning into overswingers who go after any pitch regardless of how good or bad it is. The philosophy of the coach is crucial to the player's attitude toward hitting. It is important that you display a positive, constructive approach. The players must understand what you expect of them. This teaching must start in batting practice. The hitter who allows a good pitch to go by in batting practice ought to face some mild penalty, just as the batter who swings at pitches outside the strike zone. A principle used at Lipscomb is that every pitch is a strike and fastball until proven otherwise. Every hitter has a certain type of pitch that gives him trouble. For some, it is high and inside; for others, it is low and away. With fewer than two strikes, the batter should always take this pitch. It may be called a ball; if not, he is still ahead of the pitcher. In fact, he should take any pitch that fools him with fewer than two strikes.

The hitter should always be alert for the pitch that he knows he can contact solidly. He must be thinking that every pitch is that one. When the count goes to two strikes, he should adjust by protecting the strike zone. To be this type of hitter, the player must know the strike zone. Experience and practice are the best teachers. It is very helpful to let the hitter stand at the plate against a pitcher and watch every delivery all the way into the catcher's mitt, with the catcher calling balls and strikes. During regular batting practice, the catcher should inform the hitter whenever he is swinging at balls or taking strikes.

The batter carries two types of equipment with him to the plate—mental and physical. The quality of these properties and their coordination will determine if the batter is of championship caliber.

PHYSICAL ASPECT

Selection of the Bat. The player should choose a bat that feels right to him and one that he can control. You should place great emphasis on bat control—that is, the ability of the hitter to control the bat during the hitting stroke. Many players use a bat that is too heavy or too long for them. The result is a loss of control and balance, with a consequent impairment of the all-important factor of timing.

The recommended length bat for the average hitter is 33 or 34 inches, with 34 preferred for the college hitter. Since most major league players favor this length, it stands to reason that the younger and less mature hitter should use a shorter and lighter bat, rather than a longer and heavier one.

The fact that most pitchers are fastballers places even greater emphasis on a light bat. As the season lengthens and muscles grow tired, even many big leaguers will switch to a lighter bat.

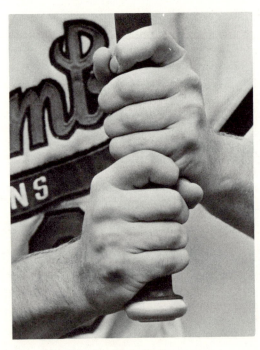

Figure 2-1

Gripping the Bat. The grip must give the hands and wrists complete freedom of movement. The bat should be gripped primarily in the fingers, not back in the palms, with the second knuckle of the top hand aligned with the third knuckle of the bottom hand (Fig. 2-1). This placement provides a more comfortable feel, allows a quicker reaction to the pitch, and produces the easy wrist action that supplies power.

Many hitters grip the bat too tightly prior to the swing. It should never be held so tightly as to whiten the knuckles. A tight grip will tense the forearm muscles and impair the swing.

Good hitting is nearly impossible without a comfortable grip that permits an explosive swing. There are three types of grips.

The *end grip* used mainly by power hitters, places the bottom hand close to or touching the knob of the bat (Fig. 2-2). This is the most common grip in baseball today.

Figure 2-2

The *modified grip* furnishes better bat control and still produces power. As shown in the photo (Fig. 2-3), the hands are placed a few inches above the knob.

The *choke grip* is used by non-power hitters who want to make contact against the overpowering fastball. As shown, the hands are placed well above the thumb (Fig. 2-4).

Stance. The stance should be comfortable, placing the batter close enough to the plate to reach any ball in the strike zone.

To determine the proper location, the inexperienced hitter may move around until he can, by bending over slightly, just touch the outside edge of the plate with his bat (Fig. 2-5). This will assure full plate coverage on a normal swing. With experience, the batter will be able to take his stance without going through this procedure.

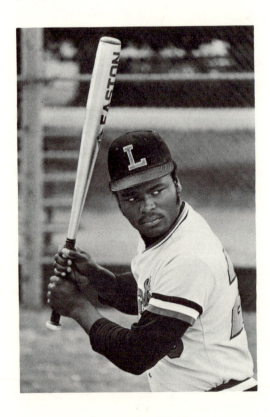

Figure 2-3

Figure 2-4

The foot spread varies from batter to batter. Many players keep their feet too close together, forcing them to lunge at the ball. This tendency can be corrected by their taking a wider initial stance. Since the stride can be only so long, a wider spread will naturally shorten the stride and help to eliminate premature striding.

Most coaches think that the spread usually should be wider than the shoulders, with the stride no longer than eight to ten inches. Many power hitters, however, take a longer stride.

The relationship of the feet to the plate is also important. There are three standard positionings: parallel, closed, and open.

In the *parallel stance*, both feet are approximately the same distance from the plate.

In the *closed stance,* the front foot is closer to the plate than the rear foot.

Figure 2-5

In the *open stance,* the front foot is farther from the plate than the rear foot.

Experimentation with these positionings may help the batter who is having trouble with specific kinds of pitches. For instance, if a player is having difficulty with the outside pitch, he may move closer to the plate and use a parallel stance. Some coaches contend that the open stance will help the batter against pitchers throwing from the same side (right vs. right, left vs. left).

Depth in the box must also be considered. Against pitchers who throw sinking fastballs and breaking pitches, a position toward the front of the box is preferred. If the hitter is standing deep in the box, he may not be able to reach the curve breaking over the outside part of the plate. Against overhand fastballers, a position toward the back of the box is favored. If the batter stands close and forward, he must hit the inside fastball far out in front of the plate to prevent being jammed.

With experience, a player will determine which stance is best for him. During the early stages, however, it is sometimes helpful to assume a spread stance. This eliminates the early step and long stride, and helps protect against pulling the body away from the plate. These faults must be corrected in order to achieve success.

Hitting Position. The hitter may swing the bat back and forth or wiggle it a few times to loosen his muscles before the swing. But, as the ball is being delivered, the bat must be brought back with the arms away from the body. Most batters hold their hands comfortably in front of their rear shoulder, with the forward arm parallel with the ground (Fig. 2-6).

Figure 2-6

Some coaches think that the front arm is the guiding arm and the rear arm the power arm. Others believe that the converse is true. Actually, it takes two strong arms to make an excellent hitter. Most players hold the rear elbow in a comfortable position slightly below the shoulder to help relax the muscles.

The hands usually are held at about shoulder height—the level that provides the *best* bat control in handling low and high pitches. Many youngsters wiggle the bat, allowing the barrel end to hang below the shoulders. This, of course, should be avoided. The bat, as well as the entire body, should be perfectly still once the pitcher begins his delivery.

Stride and Swing. In the stance, the weight is evenly distributed between both feet. As the pitcher delivers, the weight shifts to the back foot. The hips, shoulders and arms pivot back, the head remains still, the wrists are cocked, and the bat is cocked over the shoulder ready to move.

The weight shift often is made before the pitcher releases the ball. Studies show that most outstanding hitters stride to exactly the same spot on each pitch. Players who stride early in the total pitching movement usually are outstanding fastball hitters, thanks to their early step. But they are usually weak against a curve or a change-up. Since some of their weight is transferred too early, their only power must come from the arms. The body weight must never be ahead of the swing. The hitter should attempt to delay his step until the pitcher starts his arm forward to release the ball. It is important not to shift the weight forward too quickly.

The player who delays his step has no such weakness because he can hit to all fields. The batter should remember: step *to* hit, not step *and* hit. There is a great difference. If the batter does step too soon, he should keep his bat back in position so that he can swing at off-speed pitches.

In a well-coordinated swing, the weight is transferred from the ball of the back foot to the ball of the front foot. As the striding foot hits the ground, the leg braces, and the swing is made off this braced leg. This position permits the free hip movement so necessary for perfect timing.

The swing continues with a forward pivot of the hips and shoulders, and a forward thrust of the arm, so that the barrel of the bat lags behind the hands until the wrists begin to roll out in front of the plate. The arms, which are kept away from the body, supply most of the power. The shorter and more compact the swing, the better the chances of making contact.

Once the batter decides to swing at the pitch, he should get the bat moving fast, and bring his body through smoothly, releasing his full power from his wrists and hands at impact with the ball. The wrist snap is the final accelerator after the hips, shoulders, forearms, and hands have made their move. The wrists should stay cocked until the hands reach the center of the body. Then, they should uncock with lightning speed. The wrists roll over as the ball is met well out in front of the plate.

The head must be kept steady and firm, with the eyes on the ball. The ball should be followed from the pitcher's hand until it is hit (good pitch) or goes into the catcher's mitt (bad pitch). *The batter should never take his eyes off the ball.* The still head is essential since the eyes must move to track the ball. The eyes pick up the characteristic of each pitch as the ball leaves the pitcher's hand. True information about each pitch is sent to the computer (brain), where a storage of information is waiting to be used. The reaction to what the eyes see can be learned and improved. The computer is only as good as the program. You should develop a program whereby the players are taught the characteristics to look for in each pitch.

The time from the point when the batter first sees the ball to the point when he makes movement is called reaction time. Once the actual movement is started, it is called movement time. Reaction and movement time are very important to successful hitting. Baseball coaches should work hard on developing drills to improve both.

The speed of the bat also is a major factor. Many players employ a very hard swing, which often throws off their timing. A moderately hard swing, with a strong wrist action, is preferable.

A problem for many a ballplayer is how to check his swing once it has been started. It occurs when the hitter has been fooled by a pitch or decides that the pitch is not in the strike zone. It is recommended that extra pressure be applied by the top hand on the bat the instant the decision is made not to complete the swing. This procedure has proven very successful at Lipscomb. A good hitter can check his swing. If he cannot, he has a bat that is too heavy and one he cannot handle.

The Follow-Through. The follow-through should be performed naturally and smoothly without throwing the body out of alignment. If the swing has been executed on balance, the follow-through should also be on balance. Ideally, the bat should complete its arc at the middle of the batter's back. This indicates that the swing has been fairly level and full enough to assure good power.

An excellent follow-through indicates a good swing and permits a rapid break from the plate. Good hip rotation is needed to maintain balance in the follow-through. The center of gravity of the body should follow a fairly level plane throughout the swing and provide an excellent follow-through.

Hitting for Power and Line Drives. It has been contended that solid contact is the main factor in achieving power. While this is somewhat true—the batter's primary goal should be to meet the ball squarely—it is not the whole answer to maximum power. Speed is also a vital element in hitting for distance. In other words, maximum power is derived from a quick arm and hip action and the rapid acceleration of the bat at the moment of impact. Correct implementation and modification of the fundamentals will enable the player to hit with the maximum power afforded by his size, strength, and ability.

Most power hitters swing too hard. This affects their timing and balance, leading to frequent strikeouts. The consistent hitter uses a moderately hard, smooth, and basically level swing, featuring good wrist action. This type of swing will produce line drives and power hits, the ultimates in the batting act.

Hitting the Breaking Pitch. The batter nearly always must look for the fastball. If thus prepared, he can easily adjust to the breaking pitch. If he is set for the curve, the fastball can be thrown by him. Once in a while, he can look for another type of pitch, but this should be the exception, not the rule.

In certain situations, such as the start of an inning or whenever the pitcher is behind or having control trouble, the batter can definitely look for the fastball. If the pitcher is getting his other pitches over but is wild with the fast one, the batter should look for the off-speed pitches.

For most hitters, the curve presents a far tougher problem than the fastball. The batter should always *go with the curve*. If it is breaking away, he should attempt to hit it to the opposite field; if it is breaking in, he should try to pull it. If a right-hander's curve is breaking inside to a right-handed batter, he can pull it. Usually, however, the right-handed pitcher will try to keep the curve low and away from the right-handed batter. In this case, he should step toward the plate and hit to right. The same theory applies for left-handed batters facing left-handed pitchers. The batter should keep his front shoulder in as long as possible against the curve. This enable him to delay his swing and thus increases his chances of going with the pitch.

The batter must study each pitcher's curve, remembering that regardless of how much it may break, it is always slower than the fastball. He must also remember that a curve thrown at him usually will break over the plate, and the one thrown over the plate will usually break outside.

Hitters experience difficulty handling the curve because (1) they have a strong tendency to pull away from the pitch, and (2) they do not follow the ball closely all the way to the bat. If they will break these habits, they can become curveball hitters. Another point to remember is that most batters cannot hit curves merely because they do not see enough of them in batting practice. To develop championship caliber hitting, the coach must schedule adequate practice against curveball pitching.

Hitting in the Clutch. The highest accolade bestowed upon a player is that he is a "clutch hitter"—he comes through when the chips are down. The most uncomplimentary is that he is a "choke-up artist." The batter must never allow the situation to intimidate him. He must convince himself that he will get the hit. He should never go to the plate with doubt in his mind. The greater the challenge, the greater should be his determination.

MENTAL ASPECT

In addition to physical skills, the outstanding ball player possesses the great intangibles of confidence, determination, aggressiveness, courage, and concentration.

Though *confidence* alone may not make a good hitter, all the great ones have it. He must feel within himself that he is a good hitter and can hit regardless of who is pitching. He should be hoping his teammates get hits so his turn at bat will come again soon. When there are runners on base, he should be wishing he were at the plate.

Practice, desire, and ability build confidence, which in turn builds *determination*. Fierce determination brings out the best in a player, and it is absolutely indispensable in hitting.

Determination produces *aggressiveness*. The aggressive hitter is at the plate to hit, as already mentioned. He expects every pitch to be a strike and that it will be "his" pitch. This does not mean he is going after every pitch. It does mean that he is ready and eager to hit.

Courage is one of the most important traits for a good hitter. No outstanding hitter ever has been afraid of the ball. He must hang in there and be ready to hit. The alert batter can always get out of the way of the pitch.

All superior hitters have the ability to *concentrate*. When they step into the box, they shut out the crowd, the catcher, and all other extraneous factors. They concentrate on the pitcher and any telltale signs he may have for giving away his pitches. The hitter should also concentrate on the pitch, watching it into the strike zone.

The outstanding hitter is intelligent; he learns something every time he goes to the plate. He is studying the pitcher from the bench and the on-deck circle, learning to think along with him. The intelligent hitter learns when he can guess and when he must protect the plate. He is aware of game situations, where to hit the ball, and when he should be taking a pitch.

MAJOR BATTING FAULTS

Every baseball coach should have the goal, as far as hitting is concerned, to develop the most outstanding hitting team that his players' physical capabilities will allow him. All coaches dedicated to the game can achieve this goal with concentrated effort and hard work.

The coach must possess a broad knowledge of the techniques and be able to recognize, diagnose, and if possible remedy the various weaknesses to which most batters are disposed. Though some of these faults may not be entirely remediable, they can, in most cases, be treated. Both the coach and the player must be willing to devote considerable time, effort, and patience toward accomplishing this.

Following is an analysis of the most common faults observed in all types of hitters:

Overstriding. The batter stands with his feet fairly close together and then takes a long step toward the pitcher. Most batters do this to get their full power into the swing. This action would not cause much of a problem if the pitcher threw the same pitch at the same speed every time. Since he does not, he creates a severe timing problem for the overstrider. Once the batter initiates his long stride, he cannot make any adjustments. Hence, if he does not get his pitch, he can be completely fooled.

Overstriders generally have difficulty with breaking pitches and change-ups, since their stride and timing are set for the fastball. Whenever a batter steps forward for a fastball and then encounters an off-speed pitch, his weight is too far forward to assure good balance, making it difficult to meet the pitch accurately.

The remedy for overstriding is to widen the stance and take a short stride. This position prevents the weight from going forward and provides good balance. With a short stride, the arms do the work in swinging, regardless of the pitch. It is also sometimes helpful to place more weight on the front foot, especially in the early stages of the transition to a short stride.

Hitching. The batter drops his hands as the pitch approaches. This position forces him to rush his swing and to swing upward. The result usually is calamitous. Since the batter cannot level the bat as he swings, especially at high inside pitches, he will seldom get his share of base hits.

Many hitters drop their bat and then bring it back to the proper position before they swing. This, however, is merely wasted motion.

In practice, the hitcher should concentrate on swinging from the starting position without any dip of the hands. He can also hold the bat against the outer part of his shoulder and raise his rear elbow. Practice in front of a mirror should help, since the batter will be able to see his mistake. The hitcher also can help himself by concentrating on keeping his hands as still as possible.

Stepping in the Bucket. This is a common fault among beginners, usually caused by the fear of being hit. The inexperienced batter feels that he can protect himself by pulling his striding foot and body away from the plate. Though this movement may furnish some protection, it increases the difficulty of reaching the outside pitch.

Few hitters who "bail out" will ever hit for a high batting average. Those who have succeeded have moved their head and shoulders toward the pitch while pulling their front foot away from the plate. The average bucket-stepper, however, also pulls his body away.

Corrective measures have met with varying degrees of success. If fear is the problem, the batter usually is letting his imagination run away with him; if this problem is not overcome early, it can intensify. Many coaches believe that once the batter is hit by a pitch, without any ill effects, the fear will disappear. This, however, depends upon the individual's emotional makeup.

If fear is not the cause, you can help cure this fault by placing a bat behind the batter's front foot. Each time the player steps away from the plate, he will step on the bat. In time, he should develop the proper habit of stepping forward.

Back-Stepping. As the pitch is being delivered, the batter takes a step back with the rear foot, then a step forward with the front foot. The first step is completely unnecessary. It throws the body off balance by moving the body weight backward at a time when it should be steady and ready to move forward. In order to cure this fault, the batter should place more weight on the back foot in his stance.

Head Turning. Head turning on the swing causes the player to lose sight of the pitch as it approaches the plate. This is a common fault, often caused by overswinging. To overcome it, the batter must keep his head down and focus on the ball all the way to the bat (if he swings) or into the catcher's mitt (if he takes). In practice, the batter should stand at the plate and keep his head still while following every pitch all the way to the plate. Another remedy for head turning is for the batter to imagine that he is meeting the ball with his shoulders.

Lazy Wrist Hitting. The batter, often one with weak wrists, fails to pull or whip the bat around fast enough. As a result, he usually hits to the opposite field, failing to capitalize on his natural power. Wrist and finger exercises—squeezing a rubber ball daily and weight training—should be prescribed.

If the lazy hitter does possess adequate wrist strength, have him practice swinging at a heavy object, such as a medicine ball placed on a stool. He must knock the ball off the stool, a feat which cannot be accomplished unless he puts sufficient strength behind his swing and follows through well.

Locking the Front Hip. Locking the front hip during the swing produces a substantial loss of body power. Whenever the rear foot is about twice as far from the plate as the front foot, the hitter's front-hip action becomes limited. This position locks the hip, preventing maximum freedom of rotation. A limited hip action makes pulling the ball difficult and cancels the value of the follow-through. This type of batter should open his stance or step toward the pitcher when he swings, thus allowing an easy, free body action with maximum body power. A good hitter has a loose, free, easy hip rotation.

Uppercutting. This is caused by a dipping of the back shoulder and hip, and is a direct result of the modern home-run craze. Many would-be long-ball hitters would be much better off employing a level swing. While a modified uppercut is not too bad on low pitches (though it usually will produce a fly ball), it is ineffectual on high deliveries, since the bat moves across the flight of the pitch.

The uppercutter should keep his front shoulder down and swing slightly downward on the high pitch. It might also be helpful for him to raise the back elbow.

Chopping. This fault represents the opposite of uppercutting—the batter swings down on every pitch. While this is desirable on high pitches, the batter certainly should not chop every pitch. He may be able to overcome this tendency by raising his front shoulder and placing a bit more weight on his back leg. The batter's front leg should be kept straight and his weight forced into the swing.

Off-the-Heels Hitting. The batter is so eager to pull the ball that he pulls his body toward his power field by lifting his toes and pivoting on his heels. This pivot action produces a faster bat action, which is effective on an inside pitch. But since the bat and the body are being pulled away from the plate, hitting any outside strike becomes very difficult.

In addition, this movement away from the pitch toward foul territory results in a considerable loss of power. A good hitter keeps his weight on the balls of his feet (not his heels) and moves into the pitch.

Head Bobbing. Head bobbing during the stride causes the batter to lose sight of the incoming pitch by producing an up-and-down image of the ball. This fault stems from an upward push off the rear leg in starting the stride. First the head is raised and then, as the stride foot drops to the ground, it is quickly dropped. Steady vision is necessary to produce a clear image of the approaching ball. The batter should practice a short, low, smooth forward drive off the rear leg. The smooth stride and reduced body motion should result in minimal head movement.

BATTING SLUMPS

Although no one has ever run a telethon for its victims, the slump remains the most dreaded disease in batting. It strikes without warning. The batter may be hitting the ball well; then suddenly everything will go wrong. He may feel no physical change nor notice any appreciable difference in his timing, but he just cannot seem to buy a base hit.

Though its exact cause remains a mystery, a slump invariably results from some fault in technique. The hitter's timing may be off; he may be taking his eyes off the ball too soon; or, subtly, he may have changed his swing, stance, or position in the box. This change can be so slight that neither the player nor the coach may notice it.

Some coaches believe that swinging at bad pitches causes a slump. Though this certainly is a characteristic of a slump, it is not necessarily the cause. Mid-season fatigue is a more likely reason. As the season wears on, the player becomes tired and cannot cope with the demands of the game. Tired eyes may not be able to follow the pitch quickly enough to get the bat around.

With guess hitters, slumps are inevitable. The odds on guessing right are loaded against the batter. When he guesses wrong for any extended period, he becomes frustrated and confused. His problem often becomes acute. He may find it difficult to swing without guessing, but he *must* adjust in order to eliminate the basic cause of his woes.

Emotional disturbances also can affect the hitter in judging the pitch and in swinging. Poor grades, girl trouble, home problems, or any number of outside pressures can prevent the batter from concentrating fully on the job, and without such concentration he cannot be successful.

Slumps often stem from injuries. If a player cannot grip or swing the bat properly, for example, his hitting is likely to fall off. Excess weight on the hips can also produce a slump. The "hippy" player has difficulty swinging the bat far enough forward and following through, because he cannot roll his hips through early enough. He thus cannot put any power into his swing and tends to hit weakly to the opposite field.

Some players can worry themselves into a slump. They will go hitless in their first two or three at-bats and immediately begin thinking in terms of "slump." They are inclined to feel that the team's success rests entirely upon their shoulders. This type of player is mentally unable to stand the strain of daily play. Anyone who is "bugged" by failure in the early innings is unlikely to come through in the later innings.

The player who can forget a bad day at the plate is less likely to slump. He considers each game a new adventure in batting and takes his dry spells in stride, unlike the worrier who carries his previous failure up to the plate with him every time.

Unfortunately, most players cannot ignore any extended series of failures, and they worry themselves into a loss of poise. They begin swinging at any pitch on the assumption that the more they swing the better will be their chances of hitting the ball. The result is total chaos.

Most coaches are convinced that a calm and intelligent attitude is the most important factor in breaking a slump. The hitter must not lose his confidence or composure. Anger, heedless swinging, and constant guessing will not improve his average.

Staleness is probably the most common cause of a slump. The athlete who is overtrained or who is exposed to a long schedule often will lose his vigor and alertness, both physically and mentally. The immediate prescription for this sort of slump is a few days of rest.

Though there are literally dozens of ways to cure a slump, the best remedy is the proverbial "ounce of prevention." A thorough understanding of the batting process affords the best preventive medicine. A coach who can spot faults quickly and correct them can keep the hitter from becoming frustrated, thus preventing or at least shortening a slump.

Whenever a player does fall into a slump, some adjustments must be made, depending upon his individual needs and batting style. Ty Cobb, for example, did not wait until he went into a slump. Whenever he was on a hot streak, he tried to maintain his physical and mental coordination by reducing his daily batting practice. This, he felt, preserved his energy and maintained his sharp mind-body synchronization, thus helping him forestall a slump as long as possible.

Hitters who are sharp enough to recognize immediately any changes in their style are better able to solve their problems and thus check a slump. They may change their grip, choke up on the bat, use a lighter bat, or shorten their swing to achieve the desired results.

It is generally known that many big leaguers adjust the weight of their bats to their level of strength during the season, mostly to prevent slumps. Early in the season, the well rested player may use a 34- or 35-ounce bat. But as the season wears on and the bat starts feeling too heavy to swing quickly and effectively, the fatigued player often will switch to a lighter bat.

Another popular way of breaking a slump is to bunt as often as possible during batting practice. Bunting develops greater concentration in following the pitch and studying the strike zone, as the player must watch the ball longer. Bunting also places less pressure on the hitter and gives him an opportunity to relax in the box. This procedure is invaluable in getting a batter to stop chasing bad pitches.

Many slumps are initiated when the hitter starts taking his eyes off the ball a split-second too soon. Tip-off: the batter is swinging at strikes, yet is constantly missing the ball. Since he is taking his eyes off the ball as he starts his swing, he is unable to make a last-second adjustment to meet a breaking pitch.

Additional concentration on each pitch—waiting a split-second longer—may help snap a slump. By watching the ball all the way to the plate, the batter can better follow any type of pitch and is more prepared to contact it solidly.

A hitter may possibly halt a slump by taking short, easy swings in an effort to hit the ball up the middle. He should try merely to meet the ball, not kill it.

Slump-ridden players should study the opposing pitcher from the bench even more closely than usual. The hitter should know the hurler's best pitch, his preferred pitch when he is ahead or behind the batter, and his general pitching pattern. This information will increase the batter's chances of hitting the ball well.

Many players change their hitting style when they are in a slump. This is all right provided the batter goes about it intelligently. Too many players, in their frustrated state, make senseless changes. They think that any change will be for the better.

When a hitter feels that his stride is causing a slump, he can take a widespread stance and not step at all in swinging. The spread stance eliminates the stride, cuts down the swing, substantially reduces body movements and jarring, and helps the hitter follow the ball more closely.

After the batter has resumed hitting the ball solidly, he can return to his normal stride and, in most cases, he will hit well. Note: In using the spread stance, the hitter must work his arms somewhat harder to compensate for the lack of power and motion ordinarily furnished by the other parts of the body.

Continuous encouragement by the coach is imperative. Never show any sign of losing faith in the player's ability, regardless of how he may look at the plate. When a player must be benched because of a slump, discuss this situation with him fully and intelligently, attacking the problem from the hitter's standpoint. Make it clear that the benching is only temporary. This outlook will encourage the player to fight his way back into the lineup.

Wise handling has helped many a player lick a slump. Never forget that a player can be made or broken by the manner in which you, the coach, handle this problem.

POINTS TO REMEMBER

A good hitter should:

1. Select a well-balanced bat of medium weight and length.
2. Study opposing pitchers.
3. Be mentally and physically alert, but not frightened.
4. Have confidence.
5. Determine to hit the good pitch.
6. Watch the ball all the time; never take his eyes off the ball.
7. Think of nothing but hitting the ball.
8. Grip bat loosely when waiting for pitch.
9. Always be ready for fast ball.
10. Swing only at good pitches, always looking for "his pitch."
11. Know his strike zone.
12. Keep arms and elbows away from body.
13. Avoid overstriding.
14. Maintain balance and coordination.
15. Avoid lunging at the ball.
16. Swing the bat parallel to the ground.
17. Step into ball, not away from it.
18. Avoid swinging too hard.
19. Avoid hitting off his heels.
20. Avoid trying to pull an outside pitch.

3

COACHING THE LINES

Many coaches in amateur baseball fail to recognize the importance of competent base coaching. Coaching on the lines is a vital phase of the game. The judgment and alertness of coaches at first and third base play an important part in the success or failure of a team. The base coaches should have a thorough knowledge of the game and its rules. They must know also the strengths and weaknesses of their own players and learn those of the opponents as quickly as possible. The primary duties of these coaches are to give signals and assist base runners.

When analyzing the opponents for bunting possibilities, the coach should watch the catcher's throwing arm, the pitcher's motion with runners on base, and the strength of the third baseman's arm. He should know the throwing and fielding ability of the outfielders in order to take the extra base against them. If he has never seen the opposing team in action and does not have access to a scouting report, he should observe its warm-up drills.

FIRST-BASE COACH

The first-base coach, although not having to pass judgment as the third-base coach does, nevertheless has important duties.

He gives encouragement to the batter and once the ball is hit must help the batter-runner. If there is to be a play at first base, he encourages the runner to run hard and, if there is an error on the throw, signals him to go to second or to stop. If the throw is high or wide of the base, he can instruct the runner to slide by voice or hand sign.

If the ball is out of the infield, the coach should point toward second, and yell either "Make your turn," or "Go for two." He may point to second base in addition to yelling for the runner to go to second (Fig. 3-1).

Figure 3-1

If he has told the runner to go to second, the coach must watch the first baseman to see that he is not trailing him. Some teams have both the shortstop and the second baseman to go out on relays, and a runner will round second carelessly, thinking no one is covering the base. This play is used on a sure double and possible triple.

If the ball is called foul, the coach should move toward the baseline and hold up both hands, saving the batter as many steps as possible.

RUNNER ON FIRST BASE

Once the batter reaches first base and cannot advance, the coach should tell him to stay on the base until he can find the ball. This combats the hidden-ball trick. He also reminds the runner of the number of outs, the throwing ability of the out-fielders, and their positions. If none is out, he tells the runner to play safe and not take chances. The coach should advise the runner to avoid being tagged by the second baseman if a ground ball is fielded within the base line, and to break up a double play if possible by sliding into the pivot man.

When the pitcher is ready to pitch and the runner has taken his position off the base, the coach sees that the lead is in the base line and is adequate according to the speed and starting ability of the player. He should also remind the runner of the pitcher's move to first base and of the catcher's throwing habits. Left-hand pitchers are extra tricky in throwing to first base; so it is important to continually warn the runner.

Figure 3-2

When the first baseman plays on the base, the runner always knows the position of the defensive man and takes his lead accordingly. However, the coach has the responsibility of warning him when the first baseman plays back. It is necessary for the coach to face the first baseman in this situation to prevent him and the catcher from working a pickoff successfully (Fig. 3-2). The second baseman may also attempt to complete this play with the catcher when the first baseman goes in for a bunt. A catcher may attempt a similar play by circling down the base line after a ball is hit, and catching the runner after he rounds the base. If such a play is attempted, the coach must be alert and warn the runner.

CALLING FLY BALLS

If a short fly ball is hit with first base occupied, the coach calls, "Half-way" unless there are two outs. If the ball is hit deep, he can call, "Tag up," for the runner frequently can advance. This, of course, depends on the speed of the runner, the number of men on base, and the throwing ability of the outfielder catching the ball. If there is a runner on second or third base with first base occupied and he tags up, the runner on first is told to do the same, for it is often possible to advance because of a throw to third base or the plate.

If there are runners on second and third base with first base also occupied, they should tag up, while the runner at first goes two-thirds of the way down the line on deep fly balls. If the ball is caught, he returns to first base; if the ball is over the outfielder's head, he will score from that position.

The coach at first base must make decisions concerning short fly balls over the infield. The runner close to the play tags up to eliminate being doubled off, and the other runners stay off the bases the distance the ball is over the infielders so they can advance if it falls safely. All runners are told to tag up on all foul flies.

THIRD-BASE COACH

The third-base coach has duties similar to those of the first-base coach. In addition, he has the responsibility for the base runner after first base has been passed. This includes indicating to him whether he should continue on to third base or stop at second. This is necessary only when the ball is hit to right field, because the runner is able to use his own judgment when it is in front of him.

The third-base coach also has the duties of advising the runner whether to continue on to the plate or to stop at third, when he should slide at third base, and toward which side of the base he should slide.

AIDING THE RUNNER

Once the runner continues to third base, he must be guided into it. If the play is likely to be close, the coach indicates to the runner to slide by extending his arms toward the ground, palms down (Fig. 3-3). Holding the hands toward either side of the base will tell the runner to which side the slide should be made. If the throw is exceptionally wild, or if no play is being made on the runner, it will not be necessary for him to slide. The coach gives him the stop information by holding both hands in the air, with the palms toward the runner (Fig. 3-4). If the play dictates that the runner should stay directly on the base, the coach should point to it (Fig. 3-5).

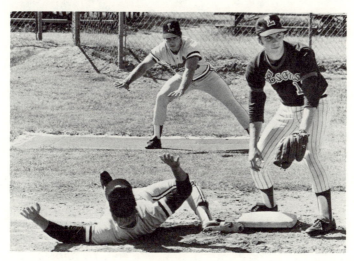

Figure 3-3

Figure 3-4

Figure 3-5

When a definite scoring opportunity presents itself, the coach runs to a point about halfway between third base and the plate and faces the player rounding third base, meanwhile watching the ball so that he can judge whether or not the player can score. The baserunner is now the sole responsibility of the coach. If he can score, the coach rotates his arms in a clock-wise motion, which is the signal for the runner to keep going. In some instances it is advisable to yell to the player to take his time. This often happens when he can easily score.

The position of the coach is especially important when the scoring opportunity is the result of a relay from the outfield or a fumble by the outfielder, because it permits the runner to be turned back even though he has rounded the base at full speed. As soon as the coach sees that the runner must be checked at third base, he runs back toward the base with his hands in the stop position (Fig. 3-6). This permits the runner to return to the base without danger of being put out. The coach also hurries back to his regular position in the coaching box after having sent a player to the plate, because he may be able to aid another runner approaching third base.

Figure 3-6

In some situations the coach may want the runner to round the base and stop. If so, he holds one hand in the air and points to the next base with his other hand.

In order to make the correct decisions at third base, it is necessary for the coach to know the speed of his players, the throwing ability of the opposing outfielders, the throwing ability of infielders who act as relay men, and the defensive positions of the outfielders prior to the ball's being hit. It is also important to consider the speed with which the ball reaches the outfield, the condition of the field, and the ability of the following batter. Other factors include the number of outs, the score, and the inning. A rule which is accepted by many third-base coaches is always to send the runner home from second on a single to the outfield with two out, because this hit may be the last scoring opportunity in the inning.

RUNNERS ON SECOND AND THIRD BASES

When a runner has reached second base and cannot advance, the coach reminds him to "find the ball." This also applies to the runner on third base. The coach tells him the number of outs and instructs him to make the line drive go through the infield if there are fewer than two outs. The coach warns the player to remain on second base if a ground ball is hit hard toward him or to his right with fewer than two outs. If there is a runner at third base, he is told what that runner intends to do. Of course, with all the bases occupied, all runners must advance on a ground ball regardless of the number of outs.

When second and third base are occupied, the coach's philosophy will determine if the runners advance on a ground ball. Many coaches tell the runners to make a ground ball go through the infield before attempting to advance. This may be good strategy with none out and the infield playing in. However, with the infield back and with one out, the runner should advance on any ground ball, except one hit directly to the pitcher. If the runner at third is thrown out at the plate, the offense has lost only one base. There would be runners at first and third bases instead of second and third, if they were held up. In a similar situation, with the infield back and third base occupied, the runner is told to score on a ground ball hit to the right side of the shortstop and in some cases a ball hit to the third baseman, depending on where he is playing.

Another important duty of the third-base coach is to watch the shortstop and the second baseman to prevent a runner on second from being picked off the base. If both the shortstop and the second baseman play in their regular positions, the coach continually calls, "All right." However, if either of them moves toward the base, he yells, "Get back." The baserunner at second should concentrate solely on the pitcher, while the coach watches both of the infielders.

On fly balls, the third-base coach follows the same rules as the first-base coach. On short fly balls, the runner plays off the base, and on long fly balls, he tags up.

The "on-deck" batter is responsible for giving aid to the runner coming home, telling him whether to stand up or to slide. He should position himself so the runner can see him clearly. This is a very important job because it directly involves a run. Also, he should clear away the bat and the mask if the catcher does not do it.

COACHES' MEETING

It is wise for the head coach to hold meetings with his base coaches from time to time before and during the early part of the season. These meetings can be used to clarify any problems and explain strategy. Coaches may discuss in confidence the players who are careless about taking signals or following instructions. A few short meetings can aid in winning many games during the season.

SIGNALS

Signals are generally used for five offensive maneuvers: the steal, take, sacrifice bunt, hit-and-run, and squeeze. Signals used should be simple and easily conveyed by a natural movement or gesture on the part of the coach. They can be given by one gesture or by a series of moves, and can be indicated by a key which precedes the sign. On some offensive maneuvers it is advisable to have an answering signal from both the batter and the runner. This prevents confusion and mix-ups in attempting plays. It is also advisable to have a sign that the batter and runner can give the coach when they are not sure what signal has been given.

The signals for all offensive plays usually come from the third-base coach. Some managers or coaches go to the coaching lines and give all the signals themselves. This, of course, simplifies the giving of signs. However, if the manager or coach remains on the bench, it is necessary for him to have a set of signals with his coaches to inform them of the particular strategy to be used. There are various ways to convey the signs to the coaches, as well as for the coaches to relay them to the batters and base runners. Any signs are workable if they are disguised. This is particularly true concerning those from the coaching lines, since the coach is in open view, and therefore a target for sign stealers on the opposing team. All signs are related to the coming pitch and usually are given after each pitch so that the coach may change his strategy to meet a different count on the batter, an advancement of a runner because of a wild pitch, or the failure of a batter to bunt the ball in fair territory. However, the sign may remain the same for the next pitch, in which case the rubbing of the uniform in a certain manner is often used to cancel the sign. It may also be necessary to take the signal off if the opposing team anticipates a steal.

SIGNALS FROM THE BENCH

Signals from the bench usually involve one hand, which simplifies the work of the coach. The following set of signs shows how the manager or coach may relay the various signals to the base coaches:

- Touching the letter on the cap—TAKE
- Touching the face with the right hand—BUNT
- Touching the letters on the uniform with right hand—STEAL
- Touching the peak of the cap with right hand—HIT-AND-RUN
- Touching the cap with two hands—SQUEEZE PLAY
- Folding the arms—DELAYED STEAL.

SIGNALS FROM
THE COACHING LINES

The previous set of signals could be used on the base line, but the base coach will need to disguise his signals, because he is in open view and a target for sign stealers, as previously mentioned. There are innumerable gestures that can be used, but the simplest combination is the key series. The set of signals below shows this series:

- KEY—Touching the face with the right hand
- SACRIFICE—Right hand to cap
- STEAL—Right hand to letters on uniform
- TAKE—Right hand on belt buckle
- HIT-AND-RUN—Right hand on pants
- SQUEEZE—Right hand to letters on cap
- TAKE-OFF (CANCEL)—Both hands on letters of uniform.

CHECKLIST FOR COACHES

1. Do not allow the runner to take his lead until the ball is located.
2. Advise the runner of the number of outs and the game situation.
3. Remind the runner of the pitcher's move to first base.
4. Advise the runner to take his lead at the proper time.
5. Watch the first baseman when he is playing back of the runner.
6. Advise the runners what to do on fly balls and line drives.
7. Alert the runner on second if an infielder sneaks in behind him.
8. Watch the second baseman in a sacrifice situation; he may sneak behind the runner at first base for a pick-off throw.
9. Inform the runner when to take a chance or when to "play it safe."
10. Know the strengths and weaknesses of the opponent.
11. Concentrate on other base runners after a runner passes the third-base coach.

12. Alert the runner if there is a possible play on him as he takes his turn at third.

13. Inform the runner if he is going on ground balls or making the ball go through the infield.

14. Concerning fly balls, inform the runner if he should try to advance or bluff a break for the next base.

15. Give all signals when both the batter and the base runner are watching.

4

DEVELOPING A POSITIVE
APPROACH TO BUNTING

With practice, any baseball player can master the art of bunting. All it takes is a little know-how and the right kind of practice. When one considers the number of games that are lost because of the failure to sacrifice a runner into scoring position, it seems that more time should be spent on this phase of the game. The main reason for the shortage of good bunters is an intense desire of coaches to go for the long ball. Consequently, little time is devoted to developing these skills.

The secret for developing excellent bunters is for the coach to supervise the bunting sessions. He must make sure the proper techniques are used and must prevent the batters from becoming lackadaisical and careless in their bunting attempts.

Another secret is for the pitcher to throw from the stretch position and put some speed on the ball. It is a mistake to lob the ball in bunting practice. The deliveries should be close to game speed so that the batter can get meaningful practice.

There are two types of bunts: the sacrifice bunt and the base hit.

THE SACRIFICE BUNT

The batter's entire concentration should center on putting the ball down in the proper spot. This must be done to ensure that the runner or runners are advanced. The batter must make the bunt before he runs to first base. He is sacrificing his out to advance the runner.

Several different shifts are available to the sacrifice bunter. The most common shift in high school is the square-around, in which the batter turns toward the pitcher by bringing his rear foot forward to a point parallel with his front foot just inside the batter's box (Fig. 4-1).

Figure 4-1

The square-around has several disadvantages. Too many young players begin shifting their position while the pitch is being made and thus are unable to follow the flight of the ball.

Also, in bringing the rear foot forward, the bunter has too much head movement and will sometimes step on the plate.

At Lipscomb and many other colleges, the players are taught a simpler (and safer) sort of shift; the batter merely pivots on the balls of his feet to face the pitcher (Fig. 4-2). This procedure does not give away his intention so quickly and involves less body movement—both distinct assets to the bunter. As the batter pivots, his upper hand slides along the bat to a position close to the trademark. It grips the bat very lightly, merely for balance, with the fingers underneath and the thumb on top (Fig. 4-3). It should be noted that the hitter must shift into position just as the pitcher's arm starts backward.

Figure 4-2

Some batters feel they can secure better bat control by sliding both hands close to the trademark, with the lower hand controlling the bat. In either procedure, the bat is held well out in front of the body at the top of the strike zone. In this position it does not have to be raised to bunt the ball. Any pitch above it will be a ball. The movement of the bat is thus always down, sharply diminishing the possibility of pop-ups.

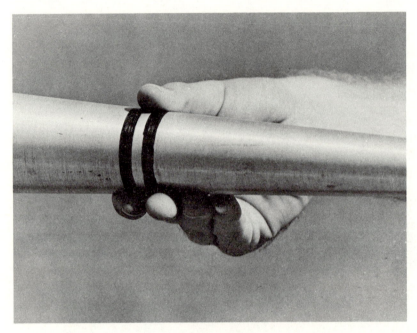

Figure 4-3

The body is slightly crouched and slightly forward, with the weight on the balls of the feet, and the bat held with the arms relaxed and slightly bent at the elbows. The bat is allowed to give when it meets the ball, the impact making it recoil a bit.

The bunter should not push at the ball, but rather allow it to hit the bat. Neither should he pull the bat back as the ball approaches, a procedure which often produces a foul ball.

The ball is bunted by raising or lowering the body from the waist and knees with as little arm movement as possible. The batter's purpose is merely to "catch the ball on the bat." The lower hand (on the handle) guides the angle of the bat. A capable bunter can place the ball toward third or first by angling the bat toward the appropriate line with the lower hand.

The placement of the sacrifice depends on the pitch, the

bases occupied, the defensive deployment, and the ability of the fielders. Unless the batter is an unusually skilled bunter, he should go with the pitch. The inside pitch, for example, should be bunted toward third base by the right-hander and toward first base by the left-hander.

With first base occupied, it is sound baseball to bunt down the first-base line. Since the first baseman must hold the runner close, he cannot leave the base until the pitcher delivers; he is thus unable to reach the ball as quickly as the third baseman. The ball should be bunted about 30 feet from the plate.

With first and second occupied, the fielding ability of the pitcher and the first baseman assumes larger significance. If the pitcher is the weaker fielder, the ball should be bunted along the third-base line. If the first baseman is the weaker, it should be bunted along the first-base line.

A team with a left-handed first baseman usually will be instructed to play for the force at third, since the left-hander can make this throw more quickly than the right-hander. This bunt is also directed to a spot about 30 feet from the plate.

If the defensive team has the pitcher breaking for the third-base line immediately after he delivers, the ball should be bunted toward the mound. Sometimes the first baseman will charge straight in. If he does, the right-handed batter can try to push a bunt past him.

When second base only is occupied, the batter should try to bunt toward the third baseman. The idea is to force him to field the ball and thus leave the base uncovered. If the pitch is outside, however, the ball may be bunted down the first-base line. The throw to third would necessitate the tagging of the runner.

Pitchers usually are advised to pitch high and inside in the bunt situations. The batter should, therefore, assume a fairly upright position so that he will be above the ball when he bunts, decreasing the danger of bunting the ball into the air.

BASE HIT

The drag bunt is a surprise attempt for a base hit as usually executed by a left-handed batter. He must conceal his intention until the last split second. As the pitcher delivers, he slides his top hand up the bat and takes a cross-over step toward first with his rear foot (Fig. 4-4). He contacts the ball on the fat part of his bat as he steps forward and tries to drag it hard enough to the left of the pitcher so that he cannot field it, thus forcing the first or second baseman to do so.

Figure 4-4

The batter must start forward with his rear foot as the pitch is in flight, and the pitch must be a good one to bunt toward the right. If it is not a good pitch for this purpose, he should let it go or try to push it down the third-base line. This may be difficult, however, if he already has started to lean toward first.

The right-handed batter's equivalent to the drag bunt is a bunt to the right of and past the pitcher, which forces the short-stop or third baseman to field the ball. This can be effective against a third baseman who is playing deep.

There are two ways to execute this bunt. First, the batter may drop the front foot back, push the top hand up the bat a short distance, and bring the handle back toward the right arm. Or, the batter may drop his rear foot back, slide the top hand forward, and push the bat handle toward the right armpit (Fig. 4-5).

Figure 4-5

SQUEEZE BUNT

There are two types of squeezes, the suicide and the safety. The *suicide squeeze* is one of baseball's most exciting plays. It is an "all or nothing" play usually employed with a runner on third and one out in a close game. With a skilled bunter, the chances of success are excellent, unless the opposition guesses right and calls for a pitchout.

The runner must not tip off the play by being overanxious— a common error in high school and college baseball. Since there is no need for more than a normal lead, the runner should not start for the plate until the pitcher's throwing hand reaches his shoulder on the forward delivery. If the runner starts at that moment, he will have no difficulty scoring on almost any bunt in fair territory. If the runner breaks too soon, the pitcher can adjust and throw an unbuntable pitch.

This also holds true if the batter squares around too soon. He must conceal his intention as long as possible. That means he should not assume bunting position until the pitcher actually starts to deliver the ball. The batter does not have to lay down a perfect bunt; all he has to do is put the ball on the ground in fair territory.

On the *safety squeeze,* the runner waits until the ball is actually bunted on the ground before racing for the plate. He should move down the line on the pitch, but not so far that he can be caught off base if the pitch is not bunted. (If the pitch is not a strike, the batter should take it.) The ball should not be bunted too hard, and it should be kept close to the foul line. The safety squeeze requires a well-executed bunt and a fast runner.

COMMON FAULTS

1. Holding bat too close to body
2. Gripping bat too tightly
3. Not starting with bat at top of strike zone
4. Not holding bat parallel to ground
5. Pivoting too late, therefore not having body under control on attempt
6. Dropping bat too soon
7. Pushing at ball
8. Bunting ball outside strike zone
9. Running to first before bunt is properly made

POSITIVE POINTS

1. Hold bat out in front of body at top of strike zone
2. Hold bat loosely
3. Keep bat parallel with ground
4. Keep head up with eyes on ball
5. Keep body slightly crouched
6. Pivot on balls of feet to face pitcher
7. Catch the ball on the bat
8. Get ball on ground before starting to first
9. Bunt only good pitches
10. Practice bunting

5

AGGRESSIVE CHAMPIONSHIP
BASERUNNING SECRETS

The secret of an outstanding, aggressive baserunning team is to instill in each player the idea that speed is not essential for success. As long as a player can start fast and think quickly, he may develop into a very good base runner. The ideal is determination, hustle and judgment with speed, a combination not found in too many athletes. Nevertheless, each player can develop the skills necessary to becoming a smart base runner.

The smart runner is always alert to the possibility of an error, the slow handling of the ball, or an inaccurate throw. He knows which outfielders have the weaker arms and tries to capitalize upon their weaknesses for the extra base.

Too many coaches wrongly assume that baserunning comes naturally to young players and that instinct alone can serve as a guide on the bases. As a result of this attitude, baserunning is one of the neglected phases of the game. Baserunning should be a major part of each team's offense—not for just a few of the players, but for the entire team. The coach must indoctrinate the team toward this goal, and each individual must be taught the aggressive approach to baserunning. Each player must have confidence and take pride in his ability to run the bases.

Practice time must be devoted to the proper techniques and fundamentals, as this will score runs, create a psychological advantage, foster confusion in the defense, and often win the close ball game. Each player must practice running properly, using good arm action, running in a straight line, and making the proper turns at each base.

In order to instill good baserunning habits, every coach should include a base-by-base tour in his teaching program.

THE START

After hitting the ball, the batter should take his first step with the back foot and go all out on his first few steps, running on his toes. He should run directly to the base and hit it in his normal stride. He should not jump for the base, since this actually adds to the time it takes to reach the base. The runner should remember to step on the middle of the base and run beyond it at full speed, slowing down gradually. He should slide only at first base to avoid a tag when the baseman has been pulled off the base by a bad throw. If the ball is fielded near the plate or along the first baseline, where the throw will come from behind him, the player must run in the three-foot lane as prescribed by the rules.

On a ball hit to the outfield, the base runner should run directly to a predetermined point that is approximately six feet short of first base and five feet to the right of the baseline (Fig. 5-1). At this point, he makes a fairly sharp pivot and crosses first base, already headed for second. The base runner should always approach the base in good position to continue to second. "Good position" means facing the next base when rounding the previous one.

A base runner always should remember that the shortest distance between two points is a straight line, and he should not waste valuable time by making two cuts while going to first base. He should touch the infield corner of the base in stride, using either the left or right foot. The important thing is to hit the base in stride (Fig. 5-2).

Figure 5-1

In rounding first it is advisable for him to run without watching the ball until the base is reached. Once there, he should try to locate the ball and determine if he can advance.

In making the turn, he should not be afraid to take a few extra steps. Some coaches teach their runners to go about a third of the way toward second, when the ball is hit to left or center field. This places extra pressure on the outfielders and, if the ball is bobbled, enables the runner to advance to second. At Lipscomb, a single is a double until the defense proves otherwise.

The aggressive runner should develop the habit of rounding the base hard, always being ready to take the extra base if the opportunity present itself. On a hit to right, the runner should not round the base quite as far, since the right fielder might throw behind him. Of course, if the batter knows he can make two bases or if the coach is pointing toward second, he should continue without hesitation.

This procedure also applies to high flies behind the infield; a hard run and a good turn will enable the runner to make

Figure 5-2

second if the ball drops in. The batter must be careful not to overtake a runner already on first base, as he will be out automatically. A similar precaution should be taken on long outfield flies, as the runner already on base might tag up in order to advance.

The coach should advise the batter on such plays. In some cases, however, the nature of the play will make it impossible for the coach to give any more definite information than "round the base." Here the runner must use his own judgment, make his turn, and proceed according to his running ability, the fielder's throwing ability, the score, the outs, and the inning.

Coaches should have their hitters run to first base as often as possible during batting practice. The coach should insist that the hitter try to accelerate quickly on every run to first base. If this is required in practice, it is likely to take place during the game.

Upon reaching first, the runner should remain on the base until the pitcher steps on the rubber. Since the pitcher must have the ball when he assumes this position, the runner's anchored position eliminates the hidden-ball trick. The runner should stand with his left foot touching the inside edge of the base, facing the pitcher and third-base coach.

At this time, the runner should receive his sign, usually from the third-base coaching box. He must be aware of the runners ahead of him, the score, the outs, the inning, and the outfielders' fielding depths. Knowledge of the outfielders' positioning, speed, and throwing ability can help a runner decide how far he can advance on a hit, whether he should tag up on a fly ball, and how far to move off the base on an outfield fly.

Each time the runner returns to his base, he should look for a signal. If he fails to receive one, he should call time or signal the coach that he does not have a sign.

The runner should take his lead by sliding his feet, rather than stepping out or crossing over. This will enable him to return quickly, if necessary. This lead must be taken *while the pitcher is receiving his signals.* The runner should not move while the pitcher takes his stretch. If he is moving toward second, he will be caught off the base if the pitcher throws to first from the top of his stretch or while coming set.

There are many kinds of leads. Some coaches teach their runners to get far enough off base so they have to dive to get back safely. Others teach the "one-way" lead. Still others favor the "two-way" lead, which puts the runner in position to move either way from a normal lead.

In the "walking" or "moving" lead, the runner begins moving off the base a little later than in the other leads, and keeps walking with short steps. If the pitcher does not force him to stop, his momentum will enable him to get a fast start for second.

Against a left-handed pitcher, it is usually wise to take a shorter lead. Since balks seldom are called on a left-hander, the runner must take extra care to see that the pitcher is throwing home before he, the runner, moves toward second.

Regardless of the type of lead he takes, the runner should always keep his eyes on the pitcher and listen for instructions from the first-base coach. Good runners study the pitcher's moves. This requires diligent concentration, but the payoff is big. The runner who knows the pitcher's moves can get a good jump toward second. He should watch the pitcher's right heel for the tip-off. If the pitcher does not lift his heel, he is throwing home. The runner should not attempt to steal if he is leaning toward first on the pitch, as he will be losing a step on his start. As the pitcher delivers, the runner should break about two or three steps so that he can advance if the ball is hit on the ground or gets away from the catcher.

The secondary movement that the base runner makes after the pitcher delivers the ball to the plate is very important to aggressive baserunning. The runner has an opportunity to take a good secondary leadoff after every pitch. This puts him closer to the next base in case the batter hits the ball. The extra step or two that the aggressive base runner takes in his secondary lead-off is the secret to heads-up baserunning, which results in winning the close games. This skill is not often emphasized in practice sessions, but it is important and can be used to great advantage in the total baserunning effort of the team.

There is no excuse for a player's being picked off a base or doubled off on a ball hit into the air. The runner should make certain not to go too far up the line.

BASERUNNING STANCE

After taking his lead, the base runner assumes a crouched position with his legs comfortably spread, feet parallel, hands off the knees, and weight on the balls of the feet (Fig. 5-3). Some players prefer to rest their hands on their knees, but most coaches prefer the hands to hang free. The only danger in this is that the runner may lean too far forward and away from the base, preventing him from getting a quick start and increasing the risk of his being picked off. Whichever stance the coach prefers, he should check in practice to see that the runners are on the balls of their feet with their weight properly balanced.

Figure 5-3

The only time the runner should be permitted to lean is on the "one-way" lead. Some coaches advocate a short lead and lean toward the next base for a steal attempt, and a long lead with a lean *back* toward the rear base if no steal is on. They believe that the runner can get a better start if he is not afraid of being caught off base, and that a runner with a long lead will bother the pitcher.

STEALING SECOND BASE

In contemplating a steal, the coach must consider the following questions: (1) Can the runner get a good start? (2) Can the hitter move the runner to the next base? (3) Is the steal worth the risk? (4) Does the situation make the play sound?

The ideal time to steal is with one or two outs, a right-handed pitcher on the mound, and a left-handed batter up. It is unwise to go with two out and a weak hitter at the plate. If the runner is out, the weak hitter will lead off the next inning. With none out, the steal is not sound baseball, as the team still has three chances to advance the runner.

The runner's first step should be a crossover—a pivot on his right foot and a step across with his left. As he runs, he should not look for the ball; he should keep his eyes on the man who is covering. The runner will know which way to slide (away from the fielder's reach) by the way he reacts to the throw.

Exception: If the pitch is hit, the runner should try to locate the ball. If he cannot, he should seek help from the third-base coach.

When the runner is going against a pitcher who is throwing with a stereotyped rhythm, he need only take a normal lead. He should start for second one count before the pitcher delivers. If the pitcher throws to first base instead, the runner should continue to second. Since the runner has a good start, it will take an accurate throw from first to get him. The runner should *always* slide into second on a steal.

BREAKING UP THE DOUBLE PLAY

In a possible double-play situation, the runner should slide into second in a way that impedes the relay to first. The rule states that a slider must have some part of his body within reaching distance of the base. This, in effect, gives him about three feet of sliding room on either side of the base.

To break up the double play, the runner must slide hard and, if possible, hook the thrower's striding foot. By watching the second baseman in infield practice and noting how he makes the pivot, the runner can know on which side of the diamond to slide.

Note: With fewer than two outs, the runner must be especially alert on a grounder to the second baseman. Too many runners allow the second baseman to tag them out and then throw to first for the easy double play.

The runner should never run into a tag play. If the infielder comes at him, he should hold up and make the man chase him, delaying (or possibly avoiding) the tag long enough to prevent the double play or allow a runner to advance.

RUNNER ON SECOND BASE

A runner on second observes a similar procedure. He stays on the base until he is sure the pitcher has the ball, while looking for signals from the third-base coach. When taking his lead, he should carefully watch the pitcher and listen to the coach for instructions on how far to get off the base and when to return.

The coach's voice will help him determine whether to return all the way to the base or only part way. This also can be determined by watching the pitcher for a pivot move.

The lead off second differs from the one off first in that the runner can move farther off the base, as it is more difficult to pick him off. The big lead, which incurs risk, really is not necessary; however, the runner should remember that he is in scoring position. A four- or five-step lead is all that is necessary, as the runner can get a *moving lead* of 25 feet on the pitcher's motion.

The steal of third usually is an unwise play. The runner is already in scoring position, and the advantage of reaching third just is not worth the risk. If the catcher cannot throw or the runner can get an exceptionally long lead, the steal can be attempted.

A steal attempt with none or one out and a left-handed batter up is considered unsound baseball. The catcher has a view of the runner and can get his throw away more easily than he could with a right-handed hitter at the plate.

The hit-and-run play is rarely attempted with a runner on second. It might be advisable with runners on first and second and a favorable count on a right-handed pull hitter who consistently meets the ball. The infielders' movements to cover the bases on the steal could leave some big holes for the batter.

The runner on second should not be caught moving back to the base as the pitcher delivers. If the ball is hit, he will lose valuable time. If the ball is not hit, he should, of course, return quickly to the base to prevent any pickoff attempt by the catcher. This habit must be developed by all runners.

On a grounder to his left, the runner should advance to third. If the ball is hit at him or to his right, he generally should return to second. Otherwise, he can easily be cut down by the shortstop or third baseman. If the ball is hit slowly, forcing the shortstop or third baseman to charge it on the infield grass, the runner usually should advance to third.

The fast and alert runner can capitalize on any mental lapse by the shortstop or third baseman. If the fielder fails to look him back to second, he may advance on the throw to first. If the fielder does look him back to second, he should not advance unless the throw is inaccurate or the first baseman has a weak arm.

On a short fly ball with fewer than two outs, the runner should assume a lead which will enable him to return to the base if the ball is caught or to advance quickly if it is not. On long flies, he should tag up and attempt to advance as soon as the fielder touches the ball.

GOING FROM FIRST TO THIRD

The runner must be aware of the outfielder's positioning and throwing ability and must discern how hard the ball is hit and where it will fall. If the ball is hit directly at an outfielder, the runner is unlikely to make third safely. If, however, the fielder must move to his right or left, the runner's chances of making third are substantially improved.

With two outs, the runner should be absolutely sure he can make third before attempting it. With one out, he can afford to take a chance. With no outs, it might not be worth the gamble, since he might take his team out of a potentially big inning.

On a single to right, the runner should look to the third-base coach *before reaching second.* The coach will be able to tell him to hold up or continue to third. An alert right fielder might throw behind the runner, hoping to catch him taking a wide turn around second.

RUNNER AT THIRD BASE

A runner at third follows the same routine as the runner at first or second. He need not look for the steal sign, however, as the steal home rarely is attempted except as the back end of a first-and-third double steal. Nevertheless, the runner must be alert for all signs, since he could be involved in a delayed steal or squeeze play.

In taking his lead, he should not go more than a step farther from the base than the third baseman. He does not want to give the baseman more than a step advantage on an attempted pickoff. The runner's lead should be in *foul territory* so that he cannot possibly be hit by a fairly batted ball.

As the pitcher starts his windup, or delivers from the set position, the runner should start toward home. The distance he goes will depend upon his judgment, but it must be long enough to enable him to get a good jump on a grounder, wild pitch, or passed ball but not far enough to be picked off by the catcher.

The runner must be leaning toward the plate when the catcher receives the ball. If he is caught returning to third, he will not be able to score on a grounder or passed ball. When returning to the base after the catcher has received the ball, he should move in fair territory.

Whenever the infield is playing normal or deep, the runner should attempt to score on any infield grounder, unless it is hit directly to the pitcher. If the infield is playing in with no outs, the runner should hold up but be alert for a possible error. With one out, a fast man can attempt to score on a slowly hit ball or any grounder which forces the fielder to move and be off balance.

The runner on third should tag up on all outfield flies and liners. If the ball falls in, he can score easily. If it is caught, he is still in position to score. On short flies which apparently will leave the outfielder with a short throw after the catch, the runner should lead off the base. If the ball is caught, he should hurry back to third. If it falls in, he will be in position to score.

In tagging up, the runner should face the field toward which the ball is hit, with one foot resting on the inside edge of the base. His body should be crouched slightly with his legs comfortably spread and his feet pointing toward the plate. As the ball nears the outfielder, the weight should be transferred to the front foot so that the first step can be made with the back foot (Fig. 5-4). This technique affords a full-step advantage over the method of pushing off with the tagging foot. The return to third on any fly ball should become reflex action. Coaches must curb the player's natural tendency to move forward on all fly balls.

Figure 5-4

THE TRAPPED RUNNER

When a runner is trapped off base, he should advance toward the next base as rapidly as possible, forcing the defense to make a good throw to get him. If the throw clearly has him beaten, he should hold up and jockey back and forth to give any other runner a chance to advance. The more times the trapped runner can force the defense to throw, the greater the chances of a bad throw. The runner always should try to work toward the next base and should run out of the baseline in a last-ditch attempt to delay the tag. Some defensive players will chase a runner even though he goes outside the prescribed line.

The trapped runner sometimes can advance by forcing a man without the ball to interfere with him. By changing direction just as the infielder makes his throw and then running straight at the thrower, the trapped runner can induce physical contact in the baseline. The umpire must call interference on this play and award the runner the next base.

When two runners are trapped, the back man should advance to the lead man's base and remain there until the lead runner returns safely. Only then should he attempt to return to his original base. Inexperienced runners often leave the base too soon, enabling the defense to tag out the lead runner and then cut down the retreating back man. Remember, when two runners occupy the same base, the original occupant is entitled to it. The other man can be tagged out.

POINTS TO REMEMBER

A good base runner should:

1. Never call himself out; wait for the umpire to make the call.
2. Always run hard, regardless of where or how the ball is hit.
3. Watch the runner ahead of him.
4. Play conservatively, if the score is close.
5. Know his opponents; watch them warm up.
6. Slide into first base only to avoid a tag by a first baseman who has been pulled off the bag.
7. Have his weight on the balls of his feet, and be sure to lean in taking his lead.
8. Remain on the base until he is sure the pitcher has the ball.

9. Never dance around while taking a lead.

10. Take his lead in a direct line with the next base.

11. Return quickly to the base after the catcher receives the pitch.

12. Know where the outfielders are playing.

13. Know the importance of his run.

14. Never allow himself to be doubled or picked off.

15. Be sure his weight is on his front foot, and facing the ball, if possible, when tagged up.

16. Avoid running into the tag on a grounder to second, when on first base.

17. Touch every base; it is there to be touched.

18. Slide into second base on all steals and double-play situations.

19. Make certain any ball hit to his right goes through before advancing from second to third base; on grounders to be left, advance immediately to third.

20. Be aggressive.

6

SECRETS OF CHAMPIONSHIP OFFENSIVE PLAY

The secret to championship offensive play is to teach the proper fundamental skills so that strategy may be successful, and to know the capabilities of the personnel with whom the coach is working. Too many young coaches approach their jobs with the impression that they can be successful by becoming outstanding strategists. This can happen only if someone has done the previous work on fundamentals that is necessary to produce a winning baseball team. Also, a coach must adjust his strategy to the capabilities of the personnel with whom he is working. This means his offensive strategy will change from year to year as his personnel changes. It is foolish for a coach to give the signal for a sacrifice bunt when the player at the plate cannot bunt.

The coach should be the only person who directs all offensive strategy. One of the reasons for this requirement is that young ball players should not carry this burden of responsibility, since they have enough to think about as they play their part in the defensive game. At times the coach will be required to direct the defense, especially when there are tying and winning runs on base. If a coach is to be successful, he should never shirk his responsibility in directing the team in all phases of the game.

The basic function of offensive play is to score runs and win ball games. To win, the coach must keep certain facts in mind at all times. They are the score, the inning, the number of outs, the strength and weakness of the defensive team, the strength and weakness of the offensive team, and the count on the batter. It is very important for the coach to be aware at all times of the status of the game.

"Percentage baseball" combines the law of averages, the chance for success, and logic. All of this weighed together will determine what will be the most sensible procedure in a given situation. No one can produce an exact percentage figure for any given stratagem. The tactic normally considered the most sound in a given situation could have the most disastrous consequences in another.

Despite the devotion of many coaches to percentage baseball, the lower the level of baseball the greater the need to deviate from it. The situation is in many cases modified by the character of a team and its opponent. What constitutes percentage baseball for one team may be suicide for another; what exploits one team's weakness could be playing right into the hands of another.

One of the first decisions a coach must make after viewing his team is what type of offensive baseball they are capable of playing. Few amateur teams are capable of combining hitting, running speed, and good defensive play.

Some coaches will attempt to score one run early in the game, hoping this will somewhat limit the opponent's offensive strategy, since the opposition must score two runs to win. If the offense can score one other run later, this will require the opposition to score three times. Many coaches in high school and college baseball believe it is imperative to get ahead as quickly as possible and then play strong defense to protect the lead.

THE SACRIFICE BUNT

The sacrifice bunt is normally used with no one out, the score close, and first base, or first and second base, occupied. Using the sacrifice bunt with a man on second base, no one out, and the game close is excellent strategy. There are at least thirteen ways to score from third base with fewer than two outs.

Some coaches will call for a sacrifice with certain players at bat, but not with others. The coach must know his players and their abilities. The use of the sacrifice depends primarily upon the personnel involved. There is great merit in being unpredictable in terms of sacrifice-bunt strategy.

The sacrifice bunt with a runner on first usually should be bunted toward first base, because the first baseman must hold the runner and will not be playing in on the grass. With runners on first and second and no one out, the best place to bunt is toward third base. The bunt should be hit fairly hard in order to prevent the pitcher from fielding it. If the third baseman is forced to field the ball, third base is left unguarded for the runner to advance from second. This situation is perhaps the most likely one for bunting in baseball.

THE HIT-AND-RUN

The hit-and-run is designed to advance a runner from first to third base with fewer than two outs. This play is not used very often in high school and college baseball because of the high level of skill required to execute it successfully.

The hit-and-run occurs with a man on first base and a right-handed batter at the plate. The runner on first breaks for second with the pitch, and the batter hits a ground ball behind the runner into right field. The play is designed to take advantage of the fact that when the runner breaks for second with the pitch, the second baseman tends to break with him to cover the base for the attempted steal. With the first baseman holding the runner at first and the second baseman moving toward second, the entire right side of the infield is open. A ground ball hit almost anywhere between first and second will get through to right field.

The hit-and-run is helpful in preventing the double play, especially with a slow man at first base. It is wise to use this play with a slow man at the plate who often hits ground balls. The author thinks the hit-and-run strategy should be used more often at every level of competition. The coach must work to develop one or two players who are capable of executing the hit-and-run with some success.

The hit-and-run play is employed to best advantage with one out and occasionally with no one out. The batter should be ahead of the pitcher on the count. Such counts as three balls and one strike or two balls and no strikes are excellent times to use the hit-and-run. If the pitcher has good control, the first pitch after a walk is a favorable time for the hit-and-run, because he will be trying to get the ball over the plate.

When the runner breaks with the pitch, it is very difficult to catch him going to second base, unless the ball is hit hard toward that base. Since one of the infielders will be moving in that direction to cover the base, he may have a play on the runner. If the ball is hit to right field, the runner usually advances to third base.

The hit-and-run play is sometimes used with only a fair hitter at bat and first and second bases occupied. Again the signal is given, and the batter attempts to hit the ball on the ground through the infield, making a double play very difficult. The first baseman usually does not hold the runner on in this situation, enabling him to get a good jump on the pitch. The third baseman is forced to cover third base, which may leave an opening at his defensive position, if he moves too quickly to cover. However, with runners on first and second and a good hitter at the plate, it is preferable to play for a base hit.

With first and third bases occupied, the hit-and-run may be used in a situation when the count on the batter is three balls and a strike or three balls and two strikes. If the pitch is a ball, the batter does not have to swing. If the ball is close to the strike zone, he should protect the runners by swinging to make contact.

In this particular situation the man on first base starts running with the pitcher's delivery to the hitter. The runner on third holds until he sees where the ball is hit. When there are no outs and the defense is in, the runner on third holds until he sees the ball go through the infield, or until an error is made.

The runner on third may attempt to score on all ground balls except one hit directly at the pitcher, with one out. If any of the infielders makes a throw to second base for a force-out, the runner at third attempts to score. The decision to remain at third or go home is based on the position of the infielders and the speed of the runner. If the infield is close, and the ball is hit sharply, the play will be on the runner at third if he breaks for the plate. If the shortstop and the second baseman are back in double-play position, the runner should attempt to score on any ground ball hit in their direction. They are giving up the run for the possible double play.

THE SQUEEZE PLAY

In the suicide squeeze play, the runner on third base breaks for the plate as the pitcher's arm starts forward to release the ball. Therefore, the runner has an excellent start toward home plate while the pitched ball is approaching the batter. The batter must bunt the ball regardless of where the pitch is thrown, since a miss will probably result in the incoming baserunner's being out. This play is usually called in a late inning, with one out and the tying or winning run on third base. A weak hitting team or one in a batting slump may play the suicide squeeze at any time provided it is not more than one run behind. A prearranged signal is given so that both the batter and the runner on third base know the play is on. In this situation it is a good idea to have the batter return a signal to the coach and the baserunner, so the runner at third does not charge toward home plate and then realize the batter has missed the signal. If the pitcher takes the set position, the suicide squeeze will work with a fast runner at third base.

The key to the suicide squeeze is the time the runner leaves third base for home plate. If he breaks too soon, the pitcher will be aware that he is going and will throw an unbuntable pitch. If the baserunner waits until the pitcher's arm starts forward to release the ball before he breaks, the pitcher will be trying to get the ball in the strike zone. This gives the batter a better chance of a good pitch to bunt.

The double squeeze is attempted with runners on second and third bases and one out. In this situation an attempt may be made to score both runners on a suicide squeeze play. As the pitcher starts his windup, the runner on second breaks for third, trying to get as fast a start as possible in order to bring himself as close to third base as he can. The runner at third base starts as explained above in the straight suicide squeeze. As the ball is bunted, the runner on second who has started for third rounds third base and continues on to the plate. It is best if the ball is bunted to the first base side of the infield to make the second baseman handle the play at first base. In doing this, the element of surprise is used against the second baseman, who is primarily concerned with covering first base.

In the "safety" squeeze, the runner on third base does not break for the plate until he is sure that the hitter has bunted the ball on the ground. If the batter pops the ball up or misses it entirely, the runner will not be out at third base. It is from this safety element that the bunt takes its name. The safety squeeze should be used primarily in the early or middle innings of a game, when there is no reason to take the extra risk that is possible with the suicide squeeze. In the late innings the opposite is true, and the squeeze becomes a much better strategy.

The element of surprise can be very crucial to the success of the suicide squeeze play. If the defense is not expecting the play, a reasonably good bunt can accomplish the mission.

THE BUNT-AND-RUN

In the bunt-and-run, the batter tries to make the third baseman field a bunted ball so that a fast runner on first base may advance all the way to third. The runner starts when the pitcher makes his move to deliver the ball to the batter. He takes his turn at second and continues on to third base as the ball is being thrown to first. If the pitch is missed by the batter, the runner goes into second base as if the play were a steal.

When the ball is bunted to the third baseman, the runner making the turn at second base must be careful of a fake throw to first base and a real throw to second.

THE RUN-AND-HIT

On the run-and-hit, the runner attempt to get an excellent jump on the pitcher, as in a steal situation. The runner on first should be fast, and he should plan to steal second if the ball is not hit by the batter.

This offensive maneuver has many features that are similar to the hit-and-run, but differs in that the batter is looking for a good pitch to hit. In this play it is not necessary that the batter be a good right-field hitter.

The run-and-hit is used quite often when there is a full count on the batter. The best time to use this maneuver is with the batter ahead of the pitcher in the count, such as two balls and no strikes.

BUNT FOR BASE HIT

The bunt for a base hit is a surprise maneuver. It can be used successfully against slow third basemen, slow-fielding pitchers, and third basemen who play deep. It should be attempted by fast runners and usually when the bases are empty. It may be tried also when the offensive team has difficulty in hitting the opposing pitcher.

The push or drag bunt is an offensive weapon which creates many problems for the defense. Speed is necessary to the success of the bunter, and this maneuver should not be attempted by those players who are slow getting down the line.

FAKE BUNT AND HIT

In some bunt situations, the defense presses the batter so closely that the possibility of success is almost negligible. When this type of defense is present, it is best to have the batter fake a bunt and hit the ball. He should concentrate on just meeting the pitch and hitting a ground ball. A good fake by the batter also may pull the second baseman toward first base, thus getting him out of position. The fake bunt and hit can best be employed early in the game or when the score is tied in the latter stages. The ground-ball double play is seldom completed in this situation.

THE SINGLE STEAL

Aggressive running teams are usually successful ones because of the extra pressure placed on the defense. The great value of the steal is that it gives the offensive team something for nothing—the advance of a runner without giving up an out.

Any discussion of the single steal usually pertains primarily to the steal of second base. This type of play is designed to move a base runner into scoring position. In amateur baseball there are many opportunities for the steal because of the throwing inaccuracy of the catchers. Also, inexperienced pitchers enhance the possibilities of the steal. The stealing of any base is a gamble of an out against a possible run on a base hit.

A steal of third is relatively rare, despite its being more easily accomplished than a steal of second. The fact that the runner can get a much longer lead and jump on the pitcher is offset by the fact that he is already in scoring position and need not risk an out by attempting to steal third.

An attempt to steal third is best undertaken with one out and a right-handed batter at the plate. This advance will put the runner in position to score on a ground ball, a fly to the outfield, an error, or a squeeze play. A steal of third with no outs is bad strategy, since there will be three chances to score the runner from second base. It is considered unsound baseball to try to steal third with a left-handed batter at the plate, since the catcher has a clear view of third and can make an unobstructed throw to that base.

It is true that bases are stolen on the pitcher, but in amateur baseball more are stolen on catchers than on pitchers.

THE DOUBLE STEAL

The double steal is employed with runners on first and third or first and second. It usually is used to best advantage with runners on first and third with one or two outs. In this situation the coach is gambling a run against an out or advancing a second runner to scoring position. The man on first breaks for second on the pitch. If the throw goes through to the base, he pulls up short and gets caught in a rundown. The man on third waits until the ball is past the pitcher before making his break for home plate. If executed perfectly, one run will score, and a runner remains on second base.

When there are runners on first and second, the best time

for the double steal comes after one out. It is important to get a runner on third base with one out. If he is thrown out at third, one runner remains in scoring position at second base with two outs.

THE DELAYED STEAL

The delayed steal is a play which should be attempted only by a base runner who possesses both speed and split-second timing. It is tried after the catcher has received the pitch, and only if the coach has noticed laxness by him in returning the ball to the pitcher or carelessness on the part of the second baseman and shortstop in moving toward the base after a pitch. If the steal is properly timed by the runner, he should take off just as the catcher starts his throw to the pitcher. The pitcher then must catch the ball and throw while the infielder who covers moves in from a deep position to make the play.

THE STEAL HOME

The steal home is a daring and foolish play in most situations. It most logically is tried with two outs and a weak right-handed batter at the plate, when the pitcher has shown carelessness in watching the runner at third base. The possibilities for success are fewer at the higher levels of baseball.

THE FORCED BALK

In the forced-balk situation, there are runners on first and third bases, two outs, and the bottom of the batting order coming to bat. The runner on first base breaks full speed towards second when the pitcher begins his stretch. The pitcher must back off the rubber if he intends to run at the base runner. If he turns towards first with his foot on the rubber, he must throw to that base, or a balk should be called. If the pitcher does not balk, and the surprise fails, the runner should continue to second base at full speed. If a throw which beats the base runner there is made to second, he should stop and force a rundown. On a throw to second or a rundown, the runner at third should attempt to score. Two good throws will be necessary to prevent his scoring.

The forced-balk works most effectively on inexperienced and nervous new pitchers. The coach should not hesitate to use this play if the percentages favor the element of surprise over the base hit.

USING THE BENCH

The wise use of the bench occasionally means the difference between victory and defeat. Using a pinch hitter in order to have a more effective batter against the pitcher is an example. In making the substitution, the coach often will delay his actions until he is sure the rival manager has decided whether to relieve the pitcher or leave him in the game. This permits the coach to select the best hitter on the bench for this particular situation. If the decision is made concerning the pinch hitter before a change of pitchers, it may be necessary to substitute a second pinch hitter, if the coach has the personnel on his bench. Then the original pinch hitter will have been used without results and lost for the remainder of the game.

If the coach has only one outstanding pinch hitter, he should be used late in the game and when the situation is most crucial. The potential pinch hitter should have ample time to warm up and have the game situation explained to him before he reports to the umpire. If a relief pitcher has entered the game, the hitter should study his motion, his speed, and his breaking pitches. If he shows signs of wildness, the batter should take a strike.

The substitution of a base runner at the right time may prove to be the decisive factor in a ball game. An astute coach foresees all game developments and always has the necessary players warming up, particularly in late innings when strategy is important.

SITUATIONS AND STRATEGY

1. Runners are on first and third bases, no one is out, and a pop fly is hit behind first. Both runners tag up, and the runner on first breaks for second as soon as the ball is caught. The runner on third starts taking a walking lead, and if the throw is made to second base, he breaks for home. If the throw is not made to second, the runner goes back to third, and there are two runners in scoring position.

2. Runners are on first and third bases with fewer than two outs, and a foul fly is hit behind the plate. Both runners should tag up, and the runner on first breaks for second. If the throw is made to second base and the defense does not have a cutoff man, the runner at third attempts to score.

3. When no one is on base, and the score is close, or the team is several runs behind, the batter should take a strike. In this situation a base on balls is as desirable as a base hit.

4. Runners are on first and second bases, no one out, and the score is close. In the early innings, strong hitters should attempt to hit. In the latter part of the game, the runners should be bunted to second and third base, provided the next batter is a good hitter.

5. A runner is on second base, score close, and no one is out. All batters should attempt to hit in the early part of the game. In the latter part of the game, if one run is needed to tie the score or to put the offensive team a run ahead, and the batter is a weak hitter, the runner may be bunted to third base. This gives the next two batters an opportunity to drive in the run.

6. A runner is on third base with one out in a late inning, and the run is crucial. The coach may use the squeeze play if the batter can bunt.

7. Runners are on second and third base with fewer than two outs in an early inning. Both runners should attempt to advance on all ground balls except one hit to the pitcher. If the runner at third is thrown out at the plate, the offensive team has lost only one base. The offensive team had runners on second and third bases before the play; if the runner is thrown out at the plate, they still have runners on first and third. This type of baserunning will put pressure on the infielders and will score runs.

8. Runners are on first and third bases with fewer than two outs.

The runner on first base should never be tagged out by the second baseman after fielding a ground ball.

9. A runner is on third base with fewer than two outs. Generally, he will attempt to score when the infield is playing back and hold when the infield is playing in.

10. A runner is on third base with fewer than two outs, and the infield playing in. On a ground ball to third base or shortstop, the runner fakes a return to third, and at the instant the infielder releases his throw to first, attempts to score. The first baseman will have to hurry his throw to the catcher, and it will take an excellent throw to get the base runner.

11. If a runner is attempting to steal a base, the batter can aid him by swinging to miss at pitches over the plate or by using the fake bunt. Sometimes this strategy will pull a defensive player out of position and also may bother the catcher in making a throw to a base.

12. If a runner is attempting to score, the player waiting his turn at bat should help by removing any equipment that is in the line of play. He acts as a coach at home plate, giving the signals to hold up or slide.

POINTS TO REMEMBER

The following points are important to the coach who is concerned with offensive play:

1. Employ an offense that corresponds with the talent of the personnel.
2. Give up an out to score a run.
3. Permit players to hit with the count 2-0 and 3-1 when runs are in scoring position.
4. Stress the importance of the sacrifice bunt, and practice this type of bunt.
5. Encourage fast men to bunt for a hit; this forces the infielders to move nearer the plate.
6. Endorse aggressive baserunning. It will pay off in the scoring of runs.

7. Use the steal according to the speed of the runners and the situation of the game.

8. Use a simple set of signals that can be understood by all members of the team.

9. Encourage all offensive players to run hard on every play. The defensive team may make a mistake.

10. Use the bench, when necessary, to win ball games.

7

DEVELOPING WINNING PITCHERS

Pitching is a skill that can be taught, if a player has the following three qualities: (1) desire to pitch, (2) ability to learn, and (3) above-average velocity on the fastball. Most pitchers fail because they have an attitude problem. They think they are doing well, and there is no reason to change their style. They will not devote enough time to practice to develop the skill necessary for success. Pitchers are successful because they are pitchers, not throwers. A thrower can become an effective pitcher, but it is a long, difficult task with you as the guide and the player working hard to follow instructions. If you have hopes of developing a winning pitching staff, you must have prospects with open minds who are eager to learn.

You must know how to get the best from your pitching staff. You may possess a tremendous amount of knowledge concerning pitching, but if you do not know methods of motivation and ways of getting your techniques across to your players, your knowledge is of little value. This is the reason great players do not necessarily make great coaches.

A coach will receive pitchers at various stages of development and with various levels of ability. It must be determined at which level to begin the instruction. You should not try to force a level of achievement upon a player. Each pitcher must be worked with individually. It is important when he is working on one segment of pitching that he should think only of it. Concentration on one skill at a time is a secret to teaching successful pitching. When the pitcher has mastered this skill, he can progress to another segment of pitching on which he needs to work.

A secret in developing a winning pitcher is for him to think positively and be aggressive. The pitcher must have the proper mental attitude toward the batter. The batter is the enemy, and the pitcher's job is to get him out. The pitcher must have confidence that he can get anyone out who carries a bat to the plate. This type of positive attitude will help develop aggressiveness, a trait that is very important to successful pitching. He must want to pitch, and he can hardly wait until he faces the next challenge. This type of attitude will help the pitcher overcome almost insurmountable odds.

Another secret that is important for you to understand is rotation of the baseball. This is a basic fundamental which is vital to outstanding pitching. The rotation or spin of the ball affects direction, and since every naturally thrown ball spins, the pitcher should know not only how it is spinning but to what degree the spin affects it. The pitcher should experiment with difficult grips to see if he can obtain more rotation as he changes the finger pressures on the ball. The thumb and the two fingers that are normally in contact with the baseball when it is gripped are the three pressure points.

Greater speed is sometimes obtained by changing finger pressure. Velocity or speed is very important to the pitcher, and he should make every effort to find the best grip. Speed in pitching comes from the long whip-like action of the arm and hand. Hand speed is very important and often overlooked by coaches. The pitcher should reach out when throwing the ball to increase hand speed and maintain a groove. Greater hand speed can be achieved with the elbow up. It is true that natural throwing speed is something with which each pitcher is born, but you can make suggestions that will enable him to get the most from his physical assets.

If it is true that pitching is approximately 75 percent of the difference between winning and losing, you will be wise to devote a major portion of your efforts toward developing a winning pitching staff.

THE TECHNIQUE OF PITCHING

The proper form and delivery in pitching are different for each individual. Most pitchers throw the ball from a three-quarter or overhand delivery, and this is the one usually taught the beginner, since it is the most natural for most players. Help the pitcher determine which is best for him, so he may reach his maximum potential. Any breaking pitches are more effective when delivered from the overhand or three-quarter position. It is not desirable to force a pitcher into the overhand pattern. A player who has been pitching with a natural sidearm or underhand delivery can sometimes make the change, but he should not unless after some practice he feels that the three-quarter or overhand action is natural and comfortable.

Many pitching coaches believe that the key to success lies in the pitcher's ability to throw the ball on a downward plane. This means that the ball follows a downward trajectory from the point of release to home plate. The greater the angle downward, the greater the advantage to the pitcher. Pitching on a downward plane means that the ball is moving in two planes, forward and down. To throw on this plane, the pitcher must throw overhand or three-quarter. If the pitcher throws sidearm, he is throwing on one plane, which is the same as the batter swinging the bat. You must work with the pitchers on keeping their elbows up to shoulder level or above. If a pitcher drops his elbow, his hand will be traveling almost parallel to the ground, and he cannot pitch on a downward plane.

One of the most common mistakes made in pitching is in the stride. As the arm comes forward to deliver the pitch, the right-hander's left leg kicks out in front of him, and his left foot is planted in the dirt in front of the mound. You must insist that the left foot come down to the left of, or just on an imaginary line from the rubber to home plate. If the foot comes down to the right, the pitcher must bring his arm down across his body, causing the loss of much of his leverage.

POSITION ON THE PITCHER'S RUBBER

Every young pitcher should learn two positions on the pitcher's rubber: the wind-up position when no one is on base, and the set position with runners on base.

Wind-up Position. To assume the wind-up position, the right-handed pitcher places his pivot foot on the right side of the rubber when facing a right-handed batter (reverse for the left-handed pitcher), with the forward spikes over its front edge and the striding foot behind it. The gloved hand hangs loosely at his side, while the ball is held in the bare hand and hidden behind the body. The eyes are on the target (Fig.7-1). When a right-handed pitcher delivers the ball to a right-handed hitter from the right side of the rubber, the hitter has very little angle on the flight of the ball; so it is difficult to judge distance.

Figure 7-1

The delivery is started with a backward swing of the arms, and the upper half of the body is bent forward. The rear foot may slide backward slightly toward second base, and the knees are slightly bent but firm. Most of the weight of the body is now on the pivot foot.

The action is now reversed as the body is straightened, and the arms are swung forward and up to a position just above the forehead. The pitcher must be careful not to block his own view of the plate with either arm. As the arms are swung upward, the pivot foot is turned outward so its outside edge is resting against the inside edge of the rubber. By placing the foot in this position, the pitcher is able to get a good balance, with a little more weight on the striding foot than on the pivot foot.

To get the maximum forward drive, the overhand pitcher should bring the knee of his free foot up high across the body as the arms swing down and back. This leg action bends and pivots the body backward as the pitcher strides forward with the free foot, and the entire body goes into the pitch like an uncoiling spring, giving the maximum power and drive. At the time of the backward bend and pivot, the pitcher keeps his eyes on the target by looking over his front shoulder. The sidearm and underhand pitcher will not lift the free knee as high as the overhand pitcher but will use a more sideward pivot.

The stride foot should be pointing toward the plate with the hips and shoulders pivoting toward the batter. All of the body actions are forward, and the ball is released with a snap of the wrist.

When the stride foot comes forward, the pitcher should land on the balls of his feet, not on the heels. Many young pitchers think that the farther they stride the harder they will throw. This certainly is not true. If the pitcher is landing on his heels, he is overstriding, and this fault will affect his body balance and control. The stride will determine where the ball will be thrown as much as any part of the delivery. Coaches should constantly be watching the pitcher's stride, especially if he has control problems.

After the pitch is released, the pitching arm comes forward and down across the body in front of the striding knee. The pivot foot pushes off and swings to a position almost parallel with or slightly ahead of the striding foot, so that the weight is well under control. Thus the pitcher is in a position to go in any direction (Fig. 7-2). If the ball is hit hard and directly at him, he can then protect himself as well as field the ball.

The motion the pitcher uses in delivering the ball should be the same regardless of the type of pitch to be made. This is important since many inexperienced pitchers often tip off the batter to what they will deliver by a slight change in action.

Figure 7-2

Set Position. The set positon is used when the pitcher must hold runners on first base, first and second base, first and third base, or all bases. Usually with the bases full, the pitcher will take the set position only when he expects the squeeze or a steal of home.

To take the set position, a right-handed pitcher places the right foot in contact with the inside edge of the pitcher's rubber and the striding foot a comfortable distance ahead toward the plate (Fig. 7-3). When holding a runner on first base, the pitcher must keep himself in a position to see the runner. This usually can be done by placing the front foot slightly toward first base. When holding a runner on second base, he should place his foot more in line with home plate (Fig. 7-4). Some pitchers keep the weight evenly distributed on both feet as they get the signs from the catcher. Others prefer to put more weight on the back foot. Whichever position is more natural for the pitcher should be used. It is important that the ball be hidden from the batter at this time.

Figure 7-3

After receiving the sign, the pitcher may stretch both arms overhead and then bring them down slowly to a comfortable position at the waist, where the hands are brought together, with the forearms parallel to the ground. The arms are relaxed against the body with the ball in contact with the throwing hand and the glove (Fig. 7-5). The pitcher should not stop his hands at the chest or below the belt. If they are held too high, he will have excess tension in the muscles of the arms. If the hands are too low, he will have to raise them higher to get started, which takes longer and permits the runner to get an extra jump.

Figure 7-4

The pitcher must be careful not to fall into a pattern of looking at the runner the same number of times or taking the same amount of time between deliveries, or the base runner who is alert will be able to get a good jump, if he desires to steal.

Usually, the throw to first base is most effective as the pitcher is bringing his hands down to the set position. If the runner is taking his lead during this period, the pitcher will catch him leaning toward second base.

Some pitchers do not stretch at all when pitching from the set position. They simply bring both hands together at the waist, pausing one second before delivering the ball. This is excellent strategy when the pitcher thinks that the runner may try to steal on the pitch. Whether the pitcher takes his stretch or not, he must remember that quickness is the key to picking men off base.

Figure 7-5

The left-handed pitcher is in a better position to hold the runner on first because he is facing in that direction when he takes his stretch. He can use the knee kick and still throw to first base or the plate. An excellent move to pick a runner off first base is for the pitcher to cock the knee, look toward first, and then toward the plate as he throws to first (Fig. 7-6).

Sometimes the pitcher can throw to the plate without the knee kick if he is expecting a steal. This maneuver will often catch the runner flat-footed and unable to get the good jump.

RUSHING

The cardinal sin committed in pitching is rushing. In rushing, the upper part of the body is ahead of the arm, and the pitcher loses all mechanical advantage; the result is tremendous strain on the arm. The weight goes forward ahead of the arm, the elbow does not have a chance to get up, and hand speed is lost. The pitcher has a tendency to throw high, and the breaking pitches are usually flat. It is impossible to get on top of the ball when the pitcher is rushing.

Figure 7-6

If the pitcher is rushing, he appears to be throwing totally with his arm and standing upright after he releases the ball. He is trying to throw the ball with his body, so he has stiffened his front leg and raised his upper body to get his arm through. When he rushes, he also bends his back too soon, and this makes him lift his body to an upright position.

It is of the greatest importance to keep the weight on the back leg longer and to try to retain the weight, while the pitching arm swings down, back and up. This gives the arm a chance to catch up to the body and allows the pitcher to throw on a downward plane.

THE BASIC PITCHES

There are three basic pitches which all pitchers should learn to throw: the fastball, the curve, and the change of pace. In professional and college baseball, other pitches are common, such as the slider and the knuckle ball, but they are not recommended for the young pitcher.

THE FASTBALL

The most important pitch for the young pitcher to master is the fastball. A fastball does not mean overpowering speed. Many pitchers capable of throwing hard never seem to fool a batter with their quickness because the ball travels in a straight line. To master the fastball, the pitcher must have control of it and the ability to make it move.

The grip is the first fundamental to be learned. The ball should be held so the fingers of the throwing hand make the best contact on the seams. The grip ordinarily will depend upon the individual pitcher, and he should experiment until he finds the one that is most efficient for him. At Lipscomb we hold the ball with the first two fingers on top and across the seams at their widest part. The thumb is underneath and the third finger along the side of the ball. The fingers should be close together, not spread apart (Fig. 7-7). The pressure points on the ball should be the center, meaty part of those two fingertips, not the extreme tips. The ball should not be gripped tightly, jammed against the inside of the pitcher's hand, but should be held with a slight air space between the ball and the hand.

Many pitching coaches have used a test to check tightness of the fingers holding the baseball. The pitcher holds it in his pitching hand with the same grip he uses in the game. The coach flicks two fingers against it, trying to knock it from the pitcher's hand. If the grip is too tight, the pitcher will retain the baseball in his hand. If the coach knocks it from the pitcher's hand, he assumes that the finger pressure is correct. If the baseball is gripped too hard or too deep in the hand, it will not sail or move. The baseball should be gripped firmly for the fastball, but the wrist should not be locked. A pitcher who grips the ball too tightly may wear blisters on his finger tips.

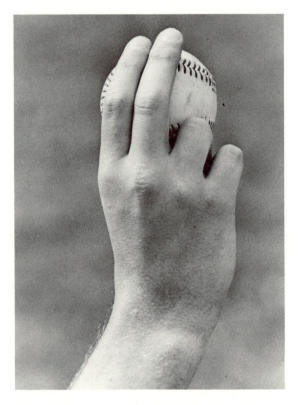

Figure 7-7

The pitcher should work continually to produce the "movement" on his fastball. This results from the release of the ball, which creates the rotation and determines the course taken by the pitch. The fastball is released off the ends of the first and second fingers, and since the second finger is longer, it will leave that finger last. Many pitchers have a natural "movement" on their fastball, and those who do not should practice releasing the pitch from the tip of the second finger on the side toward the third finger. Slightly greater pressure exerted by the second finger as the ball is released gives it the rotation that makes it hop. A definite wrist snap should be used as it is released. At Lipscomb the pitching staff has had success in making the fastball move by following through with the hand and wrist snap toward the glove hand rather than toward the ground.

The good, straight, overhand fastball has a tendency to rise because of the upward rotation of the ball on the release. The fastball from a three-quarter overhand delivery tends to rise slightly and move to the right of a right-handed pitcher.

The sidearm delivery is similar in that the ball will move toward the right if delivered by a right-handed pitcher. The rotation of the ball is sideward in the direction of release. The effectiveness of the side-armer is enhanced if the batter places his weight on his heels and leans away from the pitch. It is important that the pitch be thrown on the outside half of home plate. If it is inside, the batter has a chance to hit it, even though he is leaning away from it. This pitch generally should be kept low.

Don't attempt to throw two different types of fastballs with different grips, such as a rising fastball (across the seams) and a sinking fastball (with the seams). It sounds great, but it generally does more harm than good. Pitchers have to use different deliveries to accomplish this, and if they throw from two positions, their overall control will be less than if they had stayed with one delivery. Pitching is a groove. It is always best to throw everything from one spot.

At Lipscomb the pitching staff is instructed to throw two different speeds of fastballs, called the 90 percent and 98 percent fastballs. The regular fastball is the 90 percent, and the extra fast is the 98 percent, which will have something extra on it, but the pitcher will still have balance and body control. In the 100 percent fastball this may be lost. The outstanding pitcher usually possesses fastballs of two different speeds.

Many pitchers spend endless hours in the bullpen trying to improve their curveball and slider, generally neglecting their fastball. They feel that this pitch is just a natural gift, and they cannot improve it. This is incorrect, and you must sell the pitchers on their capabilities toward extending their abilities. Any pitcher can learn to throw his fastball harder than he ever imagined, throw it to the right spot, and throw it so it approaches the plate with "movement."

In summary, there are three major points to keep in mind when teaching a pitcher to throw the fastball: (1) *balance*— proper body balance must be maintained at all times; (2) *leverage*—to get the maximum leverage, the arm must be fully extended at the backward position; and (3) *force*—all force must be exerted on a straight line and toward the target if maximum effectiveness is to be achieved.

THE CURVEBALL

The initial grip and arm action for throwing the curveball should be identical with that of a fastball, so the pitcher does not give away the pitch before it is delivered. As the windup is started and the ball lifted over the head, the fingers slide parallel to the seam, so the middle finger has good contact along a seam. It usually is gripped more tightly with the middle finger and thumb, while the index finger merely acts as a guide. Don't grip the ball too tightly with the thumb, or the wrist snap will be restricted.

Some pitchers shift their middle and index fingers until the middle finger is on the curved part of the seam (Fig. 7-8). Others turn the hand from the back of the ball to the outside so the curved part of the seam is inside the hand and then place the middle finger along the seam. The middle and index fingers are close together, and the thumb is flat on the ball (Fig. 7-9).

As the pitching arm is brought forward and the ball is about to be released, the wrist is snapped inward. This snapping of the wrist is very important, since it causes the ball to spin faster and the curve to break sharply. The wrist must be relaxed for the pitcher to get the proper wrist snap and to utilize the entire length of his fingers. There is a downward pull as the ball comes off the surface of the middle finger and rolls over the index finger. The pitcher should be striving for all possible downward rotation on the curve, since this is what makes the ball hard to hit. A shortened stride helps the pitcher to get more break on the ball because it is easier for the arm to follow through in a downward direction. The pitcher should feel that his hand has inscribed a circle beginning where the throwing arm started forward and ending at his opposite knee.

Figure 7-8

Figure 7-9

A recommended way to get the "feel" of the curveball spin is to hold the ball without the thumb on it, jamming it back into the hand and snapping the wrist as it is released. At first the ball should be thrown only a few feet. As the pitcher gets the "feel" of the spin, he may lay his thumb back on the ball and become accustomed to longer throws, working with the catcher. Check the spin of the ball by standing directly behind the catcher. A ball that is spinning fast and about a single axis will show a small dot on its upper side. This spot is the axis around which the ball is spinning. If it is not spinning correctly, an oblong spot will show.

The pitcher should not try to throw the curveball with a crook in his arm. It should be extended as it is during a fastball pitch. The pitcher should be thinking fastball all the way in the delivery until his arm gets slightly in front of the head. The palm is facing the hitter. Then he goes to the curve by snapping the hand forward and down so that the back of the hand is facing the batter. This will give the pitcher maximum wrist action. The more the arm is crooked, the more the wrist is locked, which retards wrist snap.

An effective curveball must be thrown accurately, and this can be accomplished only through concentrated practice. The pitcher must concentrate on the spot from which the ball will start to break and on the amount of its curve. To be of any value, the curveball must be thrown below the batter's belt. High curveballs do not break as sharply as do low curveballs. The curveball thrown high permits the batter to see the spin and judge its final break while in flight. The good breaking curveball which can be thrown over the plate for a strike will make a pitcher a top winner.

Several common causes for the hanging curveball will be discussed here. Usually the pitcher who is throwing the curveball in the batter's eyes is *not pulling down hard on the ball as he comes forward with the wrist*. He should try to bring the shoulder of his throwing arm down as he releases the ball. Young pitchers have trouble *getting on top of the ball* to keep it from hanging. As mentioned earlier, the pitcher must shorten the stride to do this. It is impossible to get on top of the ball if the stride is too long. Pitchers who have trouble *bending the back* usually have trouble with the curve hanging. Other points which you must look for when the curve is hanging are *poor wrist action, releasing the ball too soon, gripping the ball too tightly, and gripping the ball too far back in the palm of the hand.*

The pitcher must remember that a wind blowing in from centerfield may cause the curve to hang or fail to break properly. A wind blowing across the plate may keep the ball from breaking sharply. Also, the curve will usually break faster in damp weather than in dry air.

The pitcher must concentrate on a low target at all times. He must concentrate, also, on bending his back and getting on top of the ball if he expects to throw the sharp curve. The excellent curve ball is a strikeout pitch if thrown below the belt. It should be kept in mind that the down-breaking curveball is a good pitch to force the batter to hit into a double play.

The secret to developing an excellent curveball is to throw overhand or three-quarter and to keep the hand ahead of the elbow. The good down breaking curveball is thrown with the elbow up. This is very important in getting the ball on a downward plane. The pitcher should not try intentionally to lead with the elbow, since this will happen in normal throwing. The hand catches up with the elbow at the release area and quickly passes it. This is where hand speed, so important to the curveball, is developed.

THE CHANGE OF PACE

The change of pace is delivered with the same body and arm action as the fastball, but it travels more slowly. In throwing the change of pace, some pitchers grip the ball as they normally do for their fastball, but they jam it farther back into the thumb and index finger, taking the fingertips off the ball as it is released (Fig. 7-10). The ball is pushed forward off the middle joints of the two fingers. To slow the ball more, the pitcher should "pull" the hand down, like pulling down a window shade.

This pitch can also be thrown by another method in which the ball is gripped loosely, well back in the palm of the hand, and then delivered with very little pressure from the fingers. Usually, three fingers are placed on top of the ball when this method is used.

A slow curve may be pitched by holding the ball very loosely and then, on release, permitting it to roll over the second joint of the first finger, as in the ordinary curveball. The fingertips should not touch the ball, and the looser the grip, the slower the pitch.

Figure 7-10

Many young pitchers like to throw the "slow curve" as a change-up pitch, which is all right if thrown at the correct speed and to the right type of batter. The pitcher should never throw a change-up to a weak hitter but should overpower him with his best pitches. The speed of the pitch must deceive the hitter, or it will be easily judged, and he will fatten his batting average. This means the pitcher must work constantly to improve his control of the pitch and develop the correct speed to go along with his other pitches.

The young pitcher should not try to throw two or three change-up pitches, since it is difficult to control a great variety of finger grips. The pitcher must remember that there must be a reason to utilize the pitch.

THE SLIDER

The slider is often called the "nickel curve," "fast curve," or "hard curve." It is usually easier to control than the curveball because it does not break as much. To the batter, it looks like a fastball, but then at the last moment it breaks away from the right-handed hitter. A good fastball pitcher can usually use the slider as his percentage pitch. It should be kept low and away to be effective, the exception being, perhaps, if the pitcher is attempting to jam an opposite side hitter.

It is best if the slider is gripped the same way as the fastball. I think the best slider is held across the seams, because the spin is harder to detect. Instruct the pitcher to grip the ball with the fingers on top, not at the side. The index finger should be raised slightly. When the index finger is raised, the ball is held off center, and the pressure is automatically applied to the inside of the middle finger. The pitcher should keep the elbow up and the weight back, bring the arm across the body, and try to keep the hand ahead of the elbow. After working with the slider and getting the feel, the pitcher should put the index finger back on the ball. Very little pressure should be applied to the ball by the index finger. Do not use stiff wrists when throwing the slider.

The slider is easily learned, and it can be thrown for a strike more consistently than the curveball. The importance of this pitch can be measured by the number of professional pitchers who use it.

SPECIALTY PITCHES

The pitcher should not add a specialty pitch without carefully analyzing his strengths and weaknesses. There must be a reason for adding the pitch. First of all, the curveball is needed along with the fastball to force the batter to deal with pitches breaking on different planes. By changing speeds on both the curve and the fastball, the pitcher forces the batter to contend not only with the different planes but also with the different speeds. The pitcher who possesses a fastball, a curve, and a change of pace has quite a repertory of weapons with which to confuse the batter. If he can get these pitches over the plate, he need not spend his time trying to develop a freak pitch.

THE KNUCKLE BALL

Of all the specialty pitches, the knuckle ball is possibly the most famous. This type of pitch probably takes the most erratic course to the plate of any thrown. It may sink, curve to either side, or jump. Its movements are highly unpredictable. These qualities make it a very difficult pitch to control. The knuckle ball rotates very little and seems to explode one way or another as it approaches the plate.

Both the overhand and sidearm pitcher may throw the knuckle ball. As in all breaking pitches, the irregular course of the ball is caused by air pressure, and the pitch is more effective when thrown into the wind or with a cross wind.

There are several methods of throwing this pitch. It can be thrown by digging the fingernails into the seams or by placing the first joints of one, two, or three fingers on the ball. Most professional pitchers who use this pitch throw the two-finger knuckle ball. It is thrown with a dead wrist similar to the change of pace, but harder. This pitch is not recommended for young pitchers.

THE FORK BALL

The fork ball is another pitch associated with pitchers of considerable experience, and the young pitcher should not attempt to master it. It can be thrown with either an overhand or sidearm delivery. The first and second fingers are spread wide, and the ball is held between them. They should not touch the seams, since the ball must slide from between them. The thumb is held underneath the ball, touching the seam. There should be a vigorous wrist snap in delivery. The fork ball usually breaks in the same direction as a curve; but with little rotation, the pitch is not predictable. Since it is normally thrown at reduced speed, it can be used effectively as a change of pace if properly developed.

THE SCREW BALL

The screw ball is held the same as a fast ball, but the actual delivery is different. The screw ball action is an unnatural movement, because the back of the hand is turned inward, toward the body, as the arm starts forward to deliver the ball. At release, the thumb pushes the ball outward as pressure is exerted by the second finger, and it leaves the hand between the second and third fingers. On delivery, the back of the hand is turned to the batter, and the arm and wrist are rolled inward toward the body. The ball may be held tightly or loosely. If it is held loosely, the pitch will have the speed of a change-up. A good screw ball pitch will break in the opposite direction from a curveball because its rotation is sideward. It is a pitch that is hard on the arm and should not be used by young players because of the unnatural arm action.

TYPES OF PITCHERS

Most pitchers may be classified in terms of their favorite and most effective pitches. Each type of pitcher approaches the game from a different point of view, and this tends to classify him.

The fastball pitcher is the one who depends primarily upon his speed in throwing the ball past the batter. The sandlot pitcher who strikes out a dozen men a game generally does it with a fastball. In college baseball, such a pitcher would be more effective if he developed a change of pace and curve. All of these pitches would require control, but the chief effectiveness lies in the difference in speed.

The curveball pitcher ordinarily has a strong hand and a flexible wrist. The key to his success is to put spin on the ball. Curveballs should be kept low; so this type of pitcher must possess better control than a fastball pitcher. Unless he happens to have a good fastball, the curveball pitcher will tend to use the fast one to set up the batter. This means the fastball will be thrown on the corner of the plate, usually low and away from the hitter.

The control pitcher is more difficult to define, but he is thought of as one who pitches to the exact spot. If his control is sufficiently sharp and he has knowledge of hitter weaknesses, he often can get by with very little "stuff." This type of pitcher does not try to strike out the batter, but he makes careful use of various speeds and techniques in delivery to keep the hitter off balance.

DEVELOPMENT OF CONTROL

It is very difficult to be a successful pitcher without control. Most pitching authorities regard control as the most important feature of pitching. Control means the ability to throw the ball to a chosen target, even if it is outside the strike zone.

The four main essentials in acquiring control are a smooth delivery, constant practice, concentration, and one release point. Though giving adequate time to practice is a simple matter, most young pitchers never learn to concentrate during this period. Excellent control without total concentration in practice is very difficult. The pitcher should have a mental picture of the course he wants the ball to follow before he starts his initial move, and he must keep his eyes on the target throughout delivery. Though it is a simple matter for him to watch the target throughout the wind-up and delivery, he often will lapse into a habit of dropping his eyes momentarily from it. The pitcher must force himself to "bear down" and to concentrate on the catcher's mitt. He should never be guilty of "going to sleep" on the pitcher's mound. He must work hard at all times. Too many pitchers try to pace themselves to finish the entire ball game and as a result lose the game in the early innings.

Poor control usually results from some "flaw" in the delivery, which can be corrected. For you to aid the wild pitcher, he must recognize the basic causes of wildness, which are listed here:

Landing on the Heel. When the pitcher strides forward, he should not land on his heel. This jars the whole body and affects his control. The stride should be made on the ball of the foot.

Aiming the Ball. This is a very common cause of poor control, especially the momentary loss of control. This usually happens in a tight situation when the pressure is great. The pitcher should not let up on a pitch to throw to a certain spot. He must believe he can get the batter out by using his best "stuff" and not aim the ball.

Taking Eyes off Target. Keeping the eyes steadily on the target has just been mentioned as an important trait in excellent control.

Throwing Across the Body. When a pitcher throws across his body, he locks his hips and impedes smooth delivery. The pitcher should open his hips by striding more to the left, if a right-handed pitcher. To stride too far to the left, however, will dissipate his power (Fig. 7-11).

Figure 7-11

Physical Tiredness. The pitcher who is in poor physical condition will weaken in his control before the game is completed. Pitching rhythm is usually affected if he becomes tired, and his control will suffer. The pitcher will have enough problems on the mound without being wild because he is not in top physical shape. The pitcher's legs are very important to him in terms of conditioning, along with the basic stamina necessary to pitch a nine-inning ball game.

Improper Body Balance. The pitcher who is off-balance during the wind-up will experience control problems. Learning to pivot and balance is vital to good control. The pitcher who can pivot and balance usually has excellent body and hip coordination. The pivot leg should be bent slightly at the knee to support the body weight as the hips are turned. The stiff leg will make it difficult to support the body weight.

Excessive Motion. The pitcher who puts too much effort into the wind-up will hinder his control. He must work to develop a smooth delivery. The no-wind-up delivery has helped several professional pitchers overcome this problem. The no-wind-up approach is recommended if the pitcher who has an exaggerated wind-up is wild. This is done by having him hold the ball in the glove in front of the belt buckle and then deliver it.

Different Arm Angle. Some pitchers use a different arm angle for every pitch. Such procedure makes it very difficult to learn a groove. For the young pitcher, it is important to throw every pitch from the same angle. If this is done, there is a better chance for him to have control.

A pitcher's position on the rubber may affect his control, even though he does not realize it. The pitcher should become accustomed to throwing from the same spot on the rubber on each pitch, and he should not move unless it is absolutely necessary. If he is throwing inside or outside of the strike zone and he cannot make other adjustments to get the ball over the plate, then he should move his pivot foot. If he consistently pitches toward the third-base side of home plate, he should move his pivot foot toward the first-base side of the rubber; if he pitches toward the first-base side, he should move his pivot foot toward the third-base side.

If the pitcher is consistently high, a slightly shorter stride in delivery will bring the ball down; if his pitches are low, lengthening the stride will bring the ball up. At the same time, the catcher should attempt to give a better target to help him. No pitcher should ever try to match the opposing pitcher's stride on the mound. This may happen if the mound is not well-kept and a hole is dug where the stride foot lands. Another pitcher may have a longer stride, and it would be a mistake to try to pitch from his "landing spot."

HOLDING A RUNNER ON BASE

RUNNER ON FIRST

Usually, the pitcher makes a throw to first base when the runner has too long a lead, or when a steal is expected. Sometimes such a throw will pick off the runner. It will at least keep him close to the base. Many inexperienced pitchers do not throw to first base often enough. If a throw is made and the runner has to slide to get back, another throw should be made immediately.

In working from the set position, many pitchers throwing to first base make a different initial move from that used in delivering to the plate. This action often tips off a base runner. An example of this is the right-handed pitcher who makes an initial move with his shoulders, arms, body, legs, or feet before pitching to the batter but lifts the right heel as the initial move to throw to first base. The base runner, by watching the right heel, will know when the throw is coming to first.

If the pitcher has a fault, he should develop and use the same initial move for the throw to first base and the delivery to the batter. This move should be slight and natural, and so coordinated with the throw to first that it cannot be called a balk.

Some pitchers have a tendency to turn their left shoulders outward toward first base, beyond the distance necessary for a proper stretch. The more the left shoulder faces first base, the greater the time needed to move it into the correct delivery position. The longer the time needed to deliver the ball to home plate, the greater the "jump" for the base runner stealing second base. The correct technique here is for the pitcher to move his eyes to see the base runner but not to move his shoulders. This also is a more effective way of seeing the target at home plate. The eyes can be moved very quickly and will not interfere with the body movement.

Unless a pitcher has been taught otherwise, he will tend to work in a definite rhythm, so much so that it can be reduced to a regular cadence count, one-two-three-four. If an alert base runner gets this count and starts his break just before the ball is delivered to the plate, he will have an excellent jump toward second base. The pitcher must vary the count in his delivery to the plate and on his throws to first base.

Many base runners develop a careless habit that an alert pitcher can take advantage of. When forced back to the base by a throw, they will lead off again as soon as the first baseman returns the ball to the pitcher. This kind of runner can be caught by a quick return throw.

If the base runner uses a crossover step in taking his lead, the pitcher can pick him off. The pitcher should time his throw to arrive just as the left foot crosses in front of the right. This places the runner in the position of taking another step with his right foot before he can recover and return to the base.

When the pitcher takes the set position and does not wish to deliver the baseball to home plate, he must remove his pivot foot from the front edge of the rubber to a position beyond the back edge of it. The pivot foot must be lifted clear of the rubber and placed on the ground behind its second base side. This must be done before the pitcher breaks his hands, to avoid committing a balk. This same procedure is used when he wishes to put the ball in play, such as on an appeal play.

When the pitcher takes the set position and the runner starts for second base, he should step off the rubber as just described and make his turn directly toward the runner. If the runner stops, the pitcher should immediately run toward him, making him commit himself toward a base. As the pitcher charges off the mound, the second baseman should run forward on the baseline ready to take a short throw. If the runner breaks toward first and the pitcher throws to that base, he should immediately back up first base on the rundown until someone else can take his position.

RUNNER ON SECOND

When there is a runner on second base, the pitcher assumes the set position before the delivery to home plate. From the set position, in a throw to second base, he should make the long turn—a right-handed pitcher turning left, and a left-handed pitcher turning right. The base runner is more likely to assume that the pitch is going to the plate than if a short turn is made. In throwing to second base, it is necessary for the pitcher to step in that direction; but he may, however, turn and make a feint to throw.

Some pitchers cannot learn to make the long turn effectively. If they cannot, they should use the short turn, which means the right-handed pitcher turns right and a left-handed pitcher turns left. If at any time the runner starts for third base and stops, the pitcher should step off the rubber and run directly at him.

When both second and third bases are occupied, and the runner on second starts for third, the pitcher should immediately step off the rubber and run directly toward the runner who left second base. He should then force the runner to third. If the runner on third base breaks for home, he should be played.

RUNNER ON THIRD

When there is a runner on third base and the score is close, the squeeze play or the steal of home is a possibility. The pitcher is the most important individual in breaking up a squeeze or steal. When a right-handed batter is at bat and the base runner makes a break for home plate, the pitcher should make his pitch at the hips of the batter. By using this type of pitch, the batter is driven away from the plate, and the catcher is in good position to tag the runner. This is also a very difficult pitch to bunt.

If the squeeze play is on with a left-handed hitter at bat, the pitch should be low and outside. This pitch is difficult to bunt and places the catcher in good position to make the tag on the runner.

The catcher and the pitcher should understand that regardless of the pitch which may have been called, when the squeeze or steal is on, it automatically is changed to a fastball unless there are two strikes on the batter. Then the pitch should remain the same and be thrown for a strike. The runner will have to slow down, since the batter must swing at the ball or be called out. If he does not swing, the catcher has a little more time and is in good position to tag the incoming runner. A change of pace should not be called if there is a possibility of a squeeze play or a steal of home.

BACKING UP BASES

You should teach your pitching staff that they have a definite defensive job to fulfill, and it is not standing on the mound. The pitcher gets in the way if he remains on the mound, and his doing so certainly shows poor coaching. The pitcher is not to act as a cutoff man on any plays. I have seen pitchers who should be backing up a base get in the way or cut off a throw that might otherwise have caught the runner.

The reason for having a pitcher back up the base is to have someone back of the infielder or catcher to stop the ball in case of a bad throw. The pitcher should be at least twenty-five feet behind any base he is backing up, and ready to block the ball to keep it from getting by and allowing the runner to take an extra base. The pitcher who backs up the play from a distance of five or ten feet is of little value.

The pitcher must be able to anticipate where a possible play may be made. He must be thinking ahead of the runner and deciding where to go in different situations.

MENTAL ASPECTS OF PITCHING

CONCENTRATION

The outstanding pitcher has learned to concentrate. This means centering his entire mental capacity on a specific objective. That specific objective is to throw the ball where he wants it to go. He cannot allow himself the luxury of letting his mind think of anything else but where he is going to throw the ball. His mind and eyes cannot wander from this definite spot.

There are other matters on which the pitcher must concentrate during the game. It is important to concentrate on throwing the ball hard and having maximum velocity on the pitch.

Concentration requires practice. Learning to concentrate includes developing the memory. To remember incidents, situations, and events is very important in being a successful pitcher. The athlete should practice developing his memory by constantly challenging his mind to perform these mental exercises.

MENTAL ATTITUDE

The proper mental attitude is a very important part of successful pitching. The pitcher must be confident that he can do the job. Confidence is developed by being successful. To be successful, he must pitch mechanically correctly and improve himself every opportunity he has to throw. As this confidence is developed, he will learn to relax.

Proper mental attitude is the basis for success in any player. It consists of the will to win, eagerness to learn, and the intelligence to retain what has been learned from experience.

EMOTIONAL STABILITY

The pitcher must work constantly on controlling his emotions on and off the playing field. Some pitchers stomp around on the field, throw things, show disgust, or sulk when things go wrong. These reactions rob the individual of the ability to concentrate.

A serious, expressionless face and a calm attitude should be constant whether things go badly or well. It is not easy to achieve these qualities, but the young pitcher should work on them.

The pitcher should not be cocky but should have confidence and be in control of his emotions. He should walk to the mound with his head up and with a look of assurance. He should not walk to the mound with lazy steps and head down. The confident attitude is important in developing the winning attitude.

THE PITCHERS' WARM-UP

One of the most important responsibilities of the pitcher is to warm up properly before the game. During this period, he not only must bring his body efficiency to its highest peak, but also must get himself ready mentally for the job ahead of him. Each pitcher must work out his own warm-up procedure, since he not only has to be ready to pitch but also must believe that he is ready.

The length of time for the warm-up depends upon the individual and the weather conditions. On a warm day, the muscles respond more quickly than on a cold one, when more pitches are required to do the job. Before a pitcher goes to the field on a cold day, his throwing muscles can be loosened by a light massage with a rubbing balm. For added warmth and protection, he should wear a wool sweat shirt.

The pitcher should not throw a ball at all until he is ready to warm up. He should start with a few close pitches and gradually move back to regulation distance. The first pitches should be easy, straight balls, with a gradual increase in speed. He should not throw hard or try any breaking pitches until he begins to sweat. Adherence to this rule will prevent injury to the pitching arm. When the pitcher feels he is ready to throw other types of pitches which will be used in the game, he again should throw easily at first and gradually increase the tempo. As this change is made from one pitch to another, the catcher should be informed.

After the first few pitches, the catcher should set his mitt as a target, about waist high and over the plate. As the warm-up progresses and other types of pitches are thrown, the target should be changed to high and low, and over the inside and outside corners of the plate. The warm-up should be completed with several breaking balls followed by four or five fastballs delivered at top speed.

Many young pitchers do not throw enough pitches from the set position during warm-up. As a result, they often lose their control in the game when they must work with men on base. After the pitcher has warmed up properly, he should throw at least one-half of his pitches from the set position.

When the weather is hot, the warm-up period should be timed so that the pitcher will have a few minutes to rest before the game starts. On cool days he may prefer not to rest after the warm-up, to eliminate any possibility of cooling off. Cold weather forces him to wear a jacket at all times, except when he is throwing.

You should keep a careful eye on your players' throwing, especially the pitching staff. Many young players are not capable of following their own judgment in warming up. They often will throw too hard too soon and too long, and develop sore arms. Warming up is an important phase of the game of baseball which cannot be overemphasized to the players.

RELIEF PITCHER'S WARM-UP

An outstanding relief pitcher is a valuable asset to any team and may win more ball games than the starters. Some teams have squad members for this particular duty, but others frequently are forced to use regular starters on their off days. So far as the actual game situation is concerned, the relief pitcher's preparation does not differ from the starter's. If he is the long relief pitcher, he should warm up sufficiently as the game starts so he can be ready with only eight or ten pitches. Whenever the game situation indicates that he is likely to be called, he immediately should begin to warm up again. This may happen several times during a game and is one of the real problems which faces relief pitchers. It is a tough assignment to get ready quickly to the point of greatest pitching efficiency after a half-dozen false starts. If the reliever must pitch from the set position when he goes into the game, he should pitch from it in the warm-up. When the relief pitcher approaches the mound, he should have all the necessary information concerning the game situation.

THE FIFTH INFIELDER

The moment the pitcher releases the ball to the batter, he becomes the fifth infielder. His ability to handle batted balls and to diagnose play situations is sometimes the difference between winning or losing. In the course of a game, he may be required to handle batted balls, cover a base, make throws to a base, and back up plays. His failure to perform any of these duties properly may cost the team the victory. The pitcher is not only the fifth infielder—he must be an efficient one.

As the ball is delivered, the pitcher brings himself into his fielding position, as described previously. If there are no runners on base and a ground ball is hit hard and directly at him, he should move off the mound after fielding the ball. This places him in better position to throw and gives the first baseman time to cover the base. The throw should never be lobbed but should be thrown with reasonable speed as soon as the first baseman reaches the base.

The pitcher should remember that on slow ground balls it is almost impossible to make a play at second or third base on an advancing runner. A good rule for most pitchers to follow is always to throw to first base any time they are pulled off the mound in fielding a ground ball, unless the catcher calls for a throw to another base.

If a ground ball is fielded by the pitcher and a base runner who has made a break stops between bases, the pitcher should play him by advancing to a point slightly ahead of him. If the pitcher can tag the runner, he should do so.

FIELDING BUNTS AND
THROWING TO BASES

If the right-handed pitcher fields a ball bunted close to the third baseline and the throw is to first, he should move quickly to a position directly in front of the ball. The right leg is braced as he stops and sets to throw in one step.

The left-handed pitcher usually fields a bunted ball close to the first baseline in front of his left foot and pivots to his right to make the throw. In many cases the pitcher's back will be toward first base as he fields a ball bunted along the third baseline, and he should pivot again to the right to make the throw.

The pitcher must be careful in fielding bunts or slow rollers, since often the spin on the ball makes it hard to handle. If it is fumbled, the throw should go automatically to first base. If the ball is fielded close to the first baseline, the throw should be made on the inside of the first base bag.

The pitcher must use good judgment on a bunt which rolls down the foul line and make the decision whether to field it or let it roll. If it does roll foul, he should slap it with the bare or gloved hand, so it will be dead.

When the pitcher fields a ground ball on which a play can be made at second base and the shortstop is covering, the throw should be a few feet to the third-base side and chest high. If the second baseman covers, the throw should be a few feet toward first-base side of second. If either infielder reaches the base before the throw starts, it should be directly to the base.

The speed with which a pitch is thrown to a base is dependent primarily upon the distance. Long throws should be hard, while shorter throws can be reduced in speed to make them easier to handle. Except under unusual conditions, the lob throw should not be used. It is often inaccurate under pressure, and the change in speed sometimes confuses the player who has to catch it. The general procedure in fielding ground balls is for the pitcher to make the shortest pivot in throwing to bases.

COVERING THE BASES

COVERING FIRST BASE

When a ground ball is hit to the left of the pitcher and he cannot field it, he should immediately move to cover first base. He should stop only if it goes through the infield or the first baseman is able to cover the base. If the first baseman can make the play himself, he should wave the pitcher off. The key to this play is for the pitcher to get off the mound quickly. It is surprising how often pitchers fail to react to a ball hit to their left. In executing this play, the pitcher should run to a spot about fifteen feet from first base and the foul line. Then he should proceed inside the line and parallel to it (Fig. 7-12). He should not watch the fielder at all until he has located the base. If he looks toward the infield too soon, he most likely will be thrown off-stride and will miss the base or be forced into an awkward position to make the catch. It is important that the pitcher receive the ball a few steps before reaching the base if possible, so he will have time to look down and make sure he touches it. If he reaches first base before the throw can be made, he should stop, placing his right foot on the inside edge of the base, and stretch out for the throw. The toss to the pitcher should be made about shoulder high and to the glove-hand side. After tagging it, he should stop quickly and turn back toward the infield if other runners are on base.

Figure 7-12

Pitchers should be taught to take nothing for granted, as the first baseman may go for a ball beyond his reach, thereby leaving the base uncovered. The pitcher must then take the throw from the second baseman.

If the ball is fielded by the first baseman and the throw goes to second base, the pitcher should run directly to first base, placing his right foot on its inside edge, and then stretch out for the throw. If a bunt or slow roller gets past the pitcher, he again should run directly to the base, making the stretch if possible. If there is not enough time, he should take the throw on the run.

COVERING SECOND BASE

If the second baseman and the shortstop both go into the outfield for a short fly ball, leaving second base uncovered, the pitcher should cover. If the third or first baseman covers that base, the pitcher takes the one which is left open.

COVERING THIRD BASE

When a runner is on second base and both the shortstop and third baseman go back after a fly ball, the pitcher should cover third base.

If first base is occupied and a bunt or a slow ground ball is hit along the third baseline which the third baseman fields, the pitcher should cover third if the third baseman cannot get back to the base, and the shortstop or the catcher fails to cover. If the catcher covers third, the pitcher should cover home plate.

COVERING HOME PLATE

When runners are in scoring position, on second or third base, and a ball gets away from the catcher, the pitcher should cover home plate. He also covers it when third base is occupied, there are fewer than two outs, and the catcher leaves his position in an attempt to catch a foul fly ball. If he fails to cover in this situation, the runner on third may easily score after the ball is caught.

In taking a throw from the catcher for a play on a runner coming into the plate, the pitcher should take a position in fair territory just in front of the plate and facing the catcher. If the throw is accurate, the pitcher will ordinarily make his turn to the right to tag the runner. Should the throw be wide, he should dive for the third-base side of home plate after catching the ball, if there is a play on the runner.

SPECIAL TIPS

Pitchers should always do their running at the end of practice, just before going into the locker room. In this way, the pitcher will not be standing around in a damp sweatshirt, risking a sore arm. It is best if all pitchers have at least two sweatshirts, which will allow them to change during the game on some occasions. Jackets should be standard equipment for all pitchers, and one should be on the field at all times, in case the pitcher needs it.

All pitchers should play plenty of "pepper" games. They help to develop quick reflexes and are excellent conditioning drills for the stomach muscles.

Many pitchers develop blisters on the fingers of the pitching hand. They are caused by pressure exerted on the ball by the fingers—especially when throwing the curveball. The fingernail is always pointed in this area. When pressure is exerted on the ball, as in throwing the curve, the point of the nail projects into the skin, causing a blister to form. This condition can be eliminated by keeping the point of the nail filed down.

PITCHING ROTATION

One of your primary responsibilities as a coach is to decide who will pitch a particular game. This decision will be made according to the dictates of the schedule. The more frequently a team plays, the more important the pitching rotation. Therefore, the professional manager is more concerned than the college, high school, or little league coach. When championships are determined by one or two games, the coach must approach every game as a crucial one. This means he must put his best pitcher against the most formidable opponent. In college and high school, he usually pitches the "ace" as often as he is physically ready to throw. It might be noted here that the coach has a responsibility to his players not to use them when they have not had adequate rest.

When rotation is being taken into consideration, the coach might do well to analyze the following:

1. The type of hitter on a particular team. Use a curveball pitcher if the opposing team likes the fastball.
2. The type of pitcher—whether he throws left- or right-handed.
3. The success that a given pitcher has had against a specific team.
4. The effectiveness of a certain type of pitcher in a particular ball park. (Fastball pitchers do better in large ball parks.)
5. The weather conditions.

There are certain peculiarities which you must consider when planning your pitching rotation. Some pitchers seem more effective in crucial games against strong teams. Other pitchers do better at night, in warm weather, or on cool days. At Lipscomb, there have been pitchers who were stronger on the road than in their own ball park. Some pitchers are slow starters and do not hit their stride until mid-season, while others start strong and tail off toward the end of the season. Others have the ability to beat one particular team consistently, while finding it difficult to beat other teams. You must pick the right man for the right situation as often as possible.

POINTS TO REMEMBER

The following are points on the fine art of pitching which each pitcher would do well to remember:

1. Always keep the eye on the target.
2. Do not rush the stride or over-stride.
3. Keep the ball in the glove until the last moment.
4. Open up and rotate the hips.
5. Be quick with the top part of the body.

6. Whip the arm through—speed it up.

7. Snap the wrist with strong hand action.

8. Wear a large glove that will help to cover up the pitches.

9. Swing the glove hand toward the hitter.

10. Follow through and try to keep the feet parallel.

11. Try to stay ahead of the hitter at all times.

12. On the day before a game, warm up lightly and get plenty of rest.

13. Wild high constantly means one of the following: overstriding, turning the ball loose too soon, or not bending the back.

14. Never pitch from the top of the pitching rubber.

15. Use as little leg action as possible with men on base.

16. Do not try to throw the curveball too hard.

17. Never deliver the ball to the plate when an infielder is out of fielding position.

18. Always cover first base on any ball hit to the left of the mound.

19. If a runner is caught off first base, always back up this base until another player takes the position.

20. Always know where the infielders and outfielders are playing.

21. Always assume the responsibility of covering any base left open.

22. Take the sign with pivot foot in contact with the rubber.

23. Practice looking a runner back at third base during the wind-up.

24. Always be sure that spikes are in good condition.

25. Back off the rubber when in stretch position, if the runner at first base disappears.

8

COACHING THE CATCHERS

Your catcher must be a leader, a take-charge type of person who can direct the play of his team. He may be compared to a football quarterback. He is one of the most important defensive players on the team. His numerous duties behind the plate—handling pitchers, calling signals, directing the defense, throwing to bases, and keeping his team informed about the game situations—contribute to the effectiveness of the pitcher out on the mound.

Aside from the above, the catcher is the only player who faces the entire field of play. He is in position to direct most of the crucial defensive plays. He must be able to make quick and intelligent decisions in all situations, which makes the catcher an important key to championship defense.

Players focus attention on him throughout the game. This means his actions and attitude can influence their thinking. The catcher must show confidence in his pitchers and strive to inspire it in his teammates. He can do this in many ways, often without uttering a word. Likewise, he can express skepticism by his mannerisms or actions. A positive attitude by the catcher is very important in a championship baseball team.

QUALIFICATIONS

One secret of a championship team is a catcher who is agile, with a sure pair of hands able to handle all types of thrown, pitched, and bunted balls. He should have a strong throwing arm that is quick and accurate. The catcher should be an intelligent athlete who is a student of the game. He must be able to analyze hitters' weaknesses and have the mental capacity to remember how each batter has been handled during the ball game. He should constantly make it a point to study each batter to learn his weaknesses.

Although he should be both mentally and physically aggressive, the catcher must also be able to remain calm under all conditions. Losing control of his emotions interferes with straight thinking and the ability to direct the ball club. The ideal catcher, in terms of temperament, is a rare combination of aggressiveness and drive with a capacity to remain relaxed. He should not be afraid of a little body contact. On many occasions the catcher will have to catch the ball, block the plate, and tag the runner who is coming full speed to the plate. Therefore, the catcher must be aggressive and have plenty of courage.

Many of the outstanding catchers have been physically large and solidly built, but there have been sufficient exceptions to prove that any kind of physique will do if a player has the proper attitude and can develop the essential skills.

POSITION BEHIND THE PLATE

The catcher's position behind the plate should be as close to the hitter as safely possible without interfering with the hitter or with his own receiving freedom. A few hitters have a tendency to step back when they swing, but the great majority step forward, bringing the bat with them. Therefore, the catcher probably can get closer to the batter than he thinks.

The catcher should keep the same distance from every batter. If the batter stands up front in the box, he should move up; if the batter stands back, the catcher will have to move back.

RECEIVING THE PITCH

There are two things the catcher must keep in mind in receiving the pitch. First, he should watch the ball all the way into the mitt (Fig. 8-1). Second, he should be aggressive, play the ball, and not let the ball play him. If he moves his mitt to soften the blow or for any other reason, the ball will miss the pocket most of the time. The catcher should reach after the ball without stretching out over the plate or interfering with the batter's swing. He should meet the ball with his mitt and catch it firmly before it moves out of the strike zone.

Figure 8-1

As a general rule, balls coming in above the knees should be caught with the glove upright (Fig. 8-2). Balls received below the knees are caught with the palm facing up (Fig. 8-3). This is a general rule. The most important thing is to catch the ball.

The basic pitches in amateur baseball are fastball, curveball, slider, and change-up. The only way to learn to catch each of these pitches is to practice. It is difficult to teach someone to catch a specific pitch, but the coach can teach the correct fundamentals and how to anticipate certain aspects of each type of pitch. This will vary with different pitchers on the same team; each type of pitch will have its own characteristics.

The catcher should expect the breaking pitch to curve or sink; if so, he will have less trouble catching it. He should always be ready for a bad pitch when the curveball is being thrown. This pitch is much more difficult to control than the fastball. If the catcher is expecting the pitch in the dirt, it will be easier to handle.

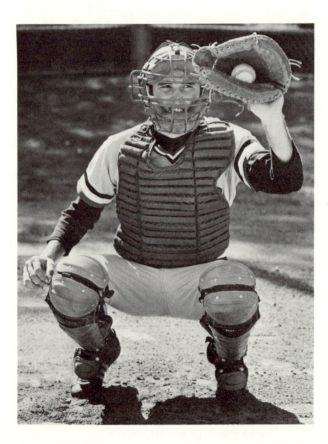

Figure 8-2

Figure 8-3

GIVING SIGNALS

The catcher's position in giving signals is a full squat from which he can survey the diamond and evaluate the situation. Giving signals is one of the catcher's arts which is sometimes underestimated. Signals are the language of the baseball field through which players communicate with each other. Those used by the catcher determine the whole defensive pattern of the game. They must be clear and simple enough to be read easily, but at the same time they must not be given in such a manner that the opposition can pick them up. Special attention should be paid to the arm and elbow, which can reveal signals unless held in the same position each time a sign is flashed. It is important that the shortstop and the second baseman read the signals, so they may be relayed to the outfielders. The first and the third basemen should check the catcher's signals from time to time, and if they can see them, the fact should be reported. A fair degree of precaution can protect the simplest of signals from detection.

There are many ways in which the catcher can give signals to his pitcher. They may be given with the right hand on the inside of the leg, well hidden in the crotch. They may be given also with the glove, and with the hands outside the crotch. Regardless of what system is used, the catcher should take a squat position behind the plate, with his feet spread comfortably, his knees apart, and his left forearm resting on the left thigh, with the glove extended beyond the knee (Fig. 8-4).

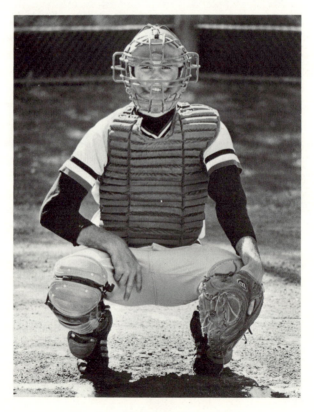

Figure 8-4

The simplest and most common type of signal used in baseball is the single series. A sample of this method is one finger indicating a fastball, two fingers showing a curve, and three fingers, a change of pace. Four and five fingers could be used to indicate other pitches or a pitchout.

In the glove series, the forearm rests on the left thigh, with the mitt extended over the knee as false signals are given in the crotch. The wrist of the mitt hand hangs loosely over the knee. When the thumb side of the catcher's mitt is pointed squarely at the pitcher, a fastball is indicated; when the palm side of the mitt shows, a curveball is signaled; when the back of the mitt is facing the pitcher, a change is indicated; when the thumb of the mitt is up, a pitchout is wanted. The glove series is excellent for night games, when it is difficult to see the single series in the crotch.

The multiple series is somewhat more complicated than the two previously mentioned. The catcher gives three consecutive signals with his fingers, and the prearranged one is the pitch to be thrown. For example, the second signal may be the prearranged sign, and the pitcher will disregard the first and third signals given. Another way of using the multiple series is to have an indicator given first to tell the pitcher which of the next signals is the pitch. For example, if he flashes two fingers first, then the pitcher uses the second sign of the next series given as the pitch. If one finger indicates a fastball, the following would be the signal for that pitch: 2-3-1-2.

In the combination series, the catcher uses some part of his catching gear in conjunction with his fingers. For example, the position of his mitt may indicate a certain number which should be added to the number given in the crotch to determine which pitch should be thrown. The mitt resting on the thigh may be one, the mitt hanging loosely over the knee is two, and the mitt in any other position would be three. These numbers then are added to the number of fingers in the crotch to arrive at the signals, which would be four, a fastball; five, a curve; and six, a change of pace. If the mitt is indicating two and there are two fingers signaling in the crotch, this would make four, which means a fastball. These signals are so difficult to steal that they practically eliminate the problem of changing signals every time a man gets on second.

After the signals for the type of pitch, the catcher should give another sign, indicating where it should be thrown, high or low, inside or out. The signal in Figure 8-5 shows the sign for a low pitch. The catcher may place his hand against the upper thigh to indicate inside or outside, depending on the side from which the batter hits.

Figure 8-5

Catching Position: The position into which the catcher moves after giving the signal depends on the pitcher and the game situation. If the pitcher is a control or curveball artist, most of his pitches will be low, and the catcher would assume a low, relaxed position. He may wish to move his feet farther apart as he crouches to receive the pitch or even drop to one knee. In this position he must be alert for a bunt, for which he is now more vulnerable.

If the pitcher depends on a fastball which is often high, the catcher obviously should assume a more upright position. When handling a pitcher who is wild, the catcher should always be in a fairly upright position, being careful to remain stationary during the pitcher's windup.

When runners are on base, the catcher must maintain a more erect position, so he will be ready to throw. His feet are spread, and he assumes a "heel and toe" alignment. The left foot is placed in front of the right by about six inches, so the heel of the left foot is opposite the toe of the right foot (Fig. 8-6). The right foot should be pointed outward slightly towards first base to facilitate shifting and throwing.

Figure 8-6

The catcher should keep his hands and arms relaxed and extended forward. A common mistake of catchers is to have their elbows between their legs in giving the target. This handicaps their ability to move the mitt to receive the ball properly. If the catcher is doing a good job, the strike that is close to being a ball will look more like a strike than a ball. The catcher is not cheating; he is making sure the umpire gets a good look at the pitch when it passes through the strike zone by stopping the ball there.

The catcher should keep his bare hand against the back of the mitt and place it over the ball after it strikes the mitt. This helps eliminate the possibility of injury to the hand or fingers from foul tips. Another method catchers often use is to keep the finger loosely closed around the thumb (Fig. 8-7). The fist should not be clenched, and the hand should be relaxed. As the ball strikes the glove, the bare hand is placed over it. No catcher can avoid getting hit on the hand with a foul tip occasionally, but he will rarely sustain anything more serious than a painful bruise if he uses this technique.

Figure 8-7

BASIC DEFENSIVE PLAYS

Throwing by the Catcher. The secret to throwing accuracy is proper body balance when releasing the ball. Quickness of the throw depends largely on how quickly the catcher can release it. A two-handed catcher will have a quicker release time, since his hand is on the ball the second it is caught. It is important for the catcher to have adequate time in practice to work on balance and quickness.

When the catcher is practicing throwing, watch for faults in placement of his feet. The basic position for any type of throwing when speed and accuracy are required is the balance on the right foot, with the left foot used as a guide. The catcher should develop the habit of throwing off the right foot.

In most situations it is desirable for the catcher to use the snap overhand throw. The overhand throw is the most accurate way to throw and is more easily handled by the infielders. Sometimes the catcher will be required to throw sidearm or underhanded. For example, if a ball is bunted or hit in front of home plate and he must hurry his throw to first or third base, he may use a sidearm or underhand snap without raising the body. Because of the distance to second base, he should use the overhand throw.

The mechanics of throwing include proper grip of the ball, coordinated arm and body movement, and the follow-through. The ball should be gripped across the seams so that it will rotate directly backwards. This type of rotation will give the ball more carry.

As the catcher receives the ball, the right hand moves over it, and the fingers feel for the seams. The fingers should be across the seams that are the farthest apart. The mitt and the ball move back toward the right shoulder as the catcher shifts his weight to his right foot. The ball is taken from the mitt before the hand reaches the shoulder and is cocked in a position above and back of the ear.

The catcher starts his throw when he shifts his weight from the right foot to the left in the direction of the target. As the ball is released, all weight should be on the left foot, with the right foot coming forward on the follow-through. The wrist should snap straight downward as the ball is released.

Dropped Third Strike. When first base is unoccupied and the catcher drops a third strike, he should always try to tag the batter after retrieving the ball. If there is no chance of tagging the runner, he should throw to first base. This should also be done with first base occupied and two outs. If there are fewer than two outs and first base is occupied, the batter-runner is automatically out. When the bases are loaded with two outs, the catcher should step on home plate for the force-out instead of throwing the ball.

No One on Base. When a ground ball is hit and fielded in the infield, the catcher should back up the throw to first base. If the throw comes from the second baseman, he backs up directly behind the throw. If it comes from the left side of the infield, he should go as far as he can, realizing he cannot get in a direct line with the throw. The right fielder should be moving in to help. The catcher should be alert to balls that may be deflected in his direction or overthrows that may bounce off the wall or fence behind first base.

Runner on First Base. When a ground ball is hit to the infield, the catcher should hold his position until he is sure the force-out is made at second base. He then moves in the direction of first base. If the ball is bunted along the third baseline and the third baseman fields it, the catcher should cover third base, if another player does not do so. This will prevent the runner from advancing from first to third on the bunt. While the catcher is moving toward third base, he should call to the third baseman to cover home plate.

Receiving Throws from the Outfielders. When the catcher is receiving throws from the outfielders, he must make every effort to catch the ball first and then tag the runner the best possible way. Since many of the throws are not accurate, he must make whatever adjustment is necessary for the tag. If possible, the catcher should always tag low.

It is not wise for the catcher to attempt deliberately to block home plate unless the runner slides. If he does slide, the catcher should drop to one or both knees and brace himself. He should tag the runner with the ball in both hands, whenever possible, gripping it very tightly in the right hand. If this is done, in case the mitt is knocked from the catcher's left hand, he still has the ball in his right hand. It should be pointed out that the catcher cannot block the plate without possession of the ball. The catcher should give the outfielders excellent targets by lining up the cutoff men correctly and by placing himself in the proper position.

On a ball thrown in from the right-field side of the diamond, the catcher should stand four or five inches from the third baseline in foul territory and close to the plate. Both feet should be parallel to the third baseline and on the third-base side of home plate, facing the throw. This position places the plate in front of the catcher and leaves it in full view of the base runner. Under these conditions the runner will normally slide to the infield side of the diamond. As the catcher takes the throw, he drops to one or both knees and makes the tag as the runner slides for the plate.

If the throw comes from the left-field side, the catcher should place his feet parallel to the first baseline, close to the front edge of the plate, and face the throw. The base runner will normally slide to the foul-territory side of the plate, since it is open to that side. As the catcher makes the catch, he drops to either one or both knees, keeping his bare hand well covered in the glove to protect it, and tags the runner.

In receiving throws from centerfield, the catcher is in a position similar to that described from left field, except that he is more nearly in front of the plate and facing in that direction.

In making the catch, he should not reach for the ball too soon, if the throw is an accurate one. If he keeps his arms at his side until the last possible moment, he can often trick the runner into slowing up slightly because he assumes there is no play. On a close play, this decoy device may be the difference between a run and an out.

On all throws wide of the plate, the catcher leaves his position and catches or blocks the ball so that no other base runner can advance. If there is a play after he has secured the ball, he should dive for the third-base side of the plate. When the throw is late and he has no play at home, he should call to the cutoff man to take the throw. At the same time, he should step into the diamond and out of the runner's way. If the cutoff man can make a play at another base, the catcher should call it.

Shifting by the Catcher. The catcher should keep his body in front of the pitch as much as possible, by shifting quickly with the foot nearer the ball. The shift should be made with the fewest possible number of steps to conserve time.

The catcher should not reach for the pitch or receive the ball flat-footed. Being a "reacher" is not consistent with outstanding catching. He should learn to shift his feet properly and get in front of every pitch whenever possible. "Reachers" have a high percentage of passed balls and missed third strikes. In shifting, the catcher will have greater success if he keeps his weight on his toes and moves his feet before moving his body.

The large glove has spoiled many catchers to the point that they do not shift their feet as much as they used to. They simply try to one-hand every pitch. The author prefers to see catchers shift, so they are in much better position to throw and block pitches not in the strike zone.

Catching Fly Balls. All fly balls in the area of home plate which can be handled by the first or the third basemen should be caught by them, since this is a very difficult play for the catcher.

The catcher should know that if a right-handed batter fouls off an inside pitch or a left-handed hitter an outside pitch, he should start back to his right. As soon as the ball is hit into the

Figure 8-8

air and the catcher sees he has a chance to handle it, he should remove his mask. He should hold it until he locates the ball and then toss it in the opposite direction from the one to which he is moving (Fig. 8-8).

The catcher should remember that a foul fly ball will always curve toward the infield because of the rotation of the ball, provided no wind is blowing. If the catcher's back is to the infield in catching a foul fly ball, he should play it an arm's length in front of him, since it will curve back toward him. The higher the fly, the greater the curve.

If a strong wind is blowing from the outfield, it will eliminate the curve, but if it is blowing toward the outfield, the curve will be greater, and the ball must be played accordingly. Whenever possible, the catcher should try to have his back to the infield on pop fly balls, so that the ball will be curving toward him. Most professional catchers say it is easier to handle the fly ball curving toward them than one curving away.

Most big-league catchers use the outfield technique when catching fly balls. The mitt is pointed upward, with the hands positioned above eye level (Fig. 8-9).

Experience is most important in catching high pop-ups, and it comes only after handling many flies during practice and games. Catching pop-ups is a matter of practice and allowing for the rotation of the ball.

Blocking Low Pitches. When falling to block pitches, the catcher should keep his body facing the ball so it will drop in front of him. On balls to the right, he pulls in the left leg and squares the mitt with the ball by bringing his left elbow in close to his body (Fig. 8-10).

High bounces which hit in front of or beside the plate are played by holding the arms down and against the body. The ball usually will rebound a few feet in front of home plate.

Low bounces are played by the catcher's dropping down on one or both knees, placing the glove near the ground, facing the ball, and trying to catch or block it with the mitt.

Fielding Bunts. When a ball is bunted in the catcher's area, he should start for it quickly. The catcher can get a faster start if

Figure 8-9

he raises his body a little higher and places his right foot a little farther back while in the receiving stance.

As he moves out for the bunt, he should flip off his mask in the opposite direction from the one to which he is going. If the ball is bunted down the third baseline and the throw is to first base, he may field it with his body to the right of the ball and his back toward first base (Fig. 8-11). On a rolling ball, he should place the left foot as close to the ball as possible, so that he will have plenty of space to field it as it rolls to his right. If it has stopped rolling, he places his right foot close to the ball, makes a turn to his left on his right foot, and then steps out with his left foot as he throws to first base. This method of fielding a ball down the third baseline helps the catcher maintain his balance. Some coaches teach that the catcher should circle to the left of the ball to make the play to first base (Fig. 8-12). This method is

Figure 8-10

acceptable but slower. If there is a possible throw to second or third base, he should keep the ball in front of him. Even though circling to the left of the ball is slower, most amateur catchers are more likely to make an accurate throw if they are facing the play.

If the ball is bunted down the first baseline and the throw is to go to first base, the catcher approaches the ball from the left side. If the throw is to second base, he runs straight at the ball. In fielding the bunt, he should place the gloved hand in front of the ball and scoop it into his mitt with the throwing hand, while remaining in a crouched position. He should use the bare hand only if the ball has stopped rolling, and it is a "do or die" play. If he has time, he should use the snap overhand throw.

Bunted balls along either baseline should be permitted to roll, whenever the batter-runner cannot be thrown out at first base. If the ball rolls foul, it should immediately be touched, so it will not roll fair. If another base is occupied, the catcher must be alert that the runner does not advance an extra base if the ball does not roll foul.

Batter Weaknesses. In working with the pitcher, the catcher will find some weaknesses common to almost all batters. The

Figure 8-11

weakness is that pitch which the batter does not hit well. A right-handed pitcher pitching to a right-handed batter usually will find him weak on one of the following pitches: a high fastball inside, a low fastball outside, or a curveball low and away. When a right-handed pitcher is pitching to a left-handed batter, the catcher will find him weak on a fastball low and outside or a curveball low and inside.

When a left-handed pitcher is pitching to a right-handed batter, he usually will find him weak on a fastball low and outside, a curveball inside and at the knees, or a fastball high and outside. When a left-handed pitcher is pitching to a left-handed batter, the catcher usually will find him weak on a curveball low and outside, a fastball high and inside, or a fastball low and outside. There are always exceptions, but these general principles do apply.

Figure 8-12

A right-handed batter who pulls the ball into left field usually hits an inside pitch well. The catcher should signal for a low, outside pitch, either a fastball or a curve. If he is a right-handed batter and hits all types of pitches to right field, he usually likes the outside pitch and probably swings late. The signal should be for a high inside pitch, since this type of batter will have difficulty getting around in time to meet the ball squarely. If the batter is left-handed and pulls the ball into right field consistently, he should be pitched low and outside. If he usually hits into left field, in all probability he will have trouble with the high and inside pitch.

The straight-away hitter may be expected to hit to either field, unless he shows other faults. It usually is preferable to keep the ball away from him, whether a curve or a fastball, with a change of pace occasionally to keep him off balance.

Spotting Batting Weaknesses. Some batters have batting habits which prevent them from hitting some types of pitches well, and it is important for both the pitcher and the catcher to spot such characteristics and to capitalize upon them. The following are examples:

A batter who crouches at the plate ordinarily will have difficulty with high inside pitches, while a batter who stands up straight may not be able to hit the low pitch consistently.

A batter whose stride pulls him away from the plate usually has difficulty hitting a low pitch on the outside corner.

A batter who lunges or overstrides usually will have trouble with off-speed pitches like the curve or change of pace. Mixing these pitches will keep him off-stride. When throwing the fastball, keep it high and tight.

A batter who steps in toward the plate on his stride often cannot consistently hit a fastball high and inside.

A batter who is "nervous" at the plate, with a tendency to swing his bat back and forth repeatedly, is vulnerable to the waiting treatment. One who is particularly tense will tend to grip the bat so tightly that his knuckles will be white. A catcher who spots this often will find a curveball or change of pace effective.

Sizing up a specific hitter's weaknesses is an art in itself. The principles given will help the catcher to some degree, but experience will be the best teacher for both the pitcher and the catcher. The battery (catcher and pitcher) should take advantage of every opportunity to watch batters hit, even their own teammates.

The Catcher and Pitcher Working Together. The catcher must know the characteristics of each of the pitchers he will catch. Every pitcher has a type of pitch upon which he relies and in which he has confidence. Whatever it may be, it is an important part of his equipment, since he believes in it. One of the first jobs the catcher must perform when practice begins is to learn the most effective pitch of each of the hurlers.

Many pitchers, when in a tight situation, will tend to rely heavily upon their favorite pitch. But when there are runners in scoring position and the batter has a known weakness, the catcher may prefer to pitch to that weakness instead of using the pitcher's favorite.

Confidence in each other is an important characteristic of an outstanding battery. If the catcher has experience and the pitcher is young, he should accept the signals given. There should be no great disagreement in calling pitches. On an occasion when the pitcher feels he can do a better job with a different pitch than the one which the catcher has called, that should be his privilege. The pitcher and the catcher should make every effort to understand each other. This is important to the relationship that should exist between them. The catcher is in the position of team leader, and most of the responsibility for a good working relationship is in his hands.

The Pitchout. The good pitchout is a pitch thrown in such a way that it is impossible for the batter to hit it. At the same time, it sets up the catcher to make a throw or gives him clearance to make a play at the plate, depending on the situation.

If the pitchout is called for a pickoff throw from the catcher to any base, it normally should be used only when there is an excellent chance of getting the runner. The game situation will determine if a pitchout should be called. Some coaches do not like it to be used unless there are two outs. They believe that with fewer than two outs a wild throw will advance the runner, and his chance of scoring becomes greater, since more batters will have an opportunity to drive him in.

When the catcher's team is one or more runs ahead, the opposition is not likely to take chances. The logical play, therefore, is to get the hitter, since the runners will be playing safe. When the defense is a run or more behind, pickoffs should be attempted only if the catcher is sure he can get the runner. If he does not throw well, the pickoff should not be attempted, since a wild throw will give the opposing team an even greater margin.

The pitchout also is used when a player is intentionally put on base with a deliberate base on balls. In this situation, the pitch should be kept outside, where the batter cannot hit the ball without stepping on the plate. The catcher must stay in his box until the pitcher releases the ball. When an intentional pass is given a right-handed batter, the catcher should stand as far right in the box as possible. As the pitch is released, he steps to the right to make the catch. The procedure is reversed on a left-handed batter.

POINTS TO REMEMBER

The following points are tips for catchers:

1. Remember the catcher must be a take-charge man and a real hustler.
2. Provide a steady target, and catch the ball as close to the plate as possible.
3. Know the pitchers' strengths and weaknesses.
4. Call all plays in front of the plate.
5. Try to catch the latter part of a pitcher's pre-game warm-up.
6. Use a wider stance if the pitcher is wild.
7. Remember to control the speed at which the pitcher works.
8. Catch high pitches from above and bring them down.
9. Do not block the umpire's vision in catching high pitches.
10. Stay as close to the batter as possible with men on base.
11. Take only one step when throwing to a base unless it is a bad pitch.
12. Never make a random throw to a base.
13. Always put on a play with an infielder when signaling for a pitchout.
14. Make the throw to third base on the inside of the diamond.
15. Cover home correctly on throws from the outfield.
16. Keep the body square to the diamond on low pitches.
17. Expect every pitch thrown to be a wild pitch.
18. Study each batter for weaknesses and catalogue them in the mind.

19. Check the defensive position of the infielders and outfielders frequently.

20. Wear catching equipment during infield practice, since it must be worn in the game.

21. Do not block home plate without possession of the ball.

22. Back up throws to first base with no one on base.

23. Remember that trouble in throwing may be attributed to foot movement and to the body being off balance.

24. Pick up bunts with two hands, scooping the ball into the mitt.

25. Bring the mitt up to the shoulder when throwing.

9

CHAMPIONSHIP FIRST-BASE PLAY

One of the most beautiful sights in baseball is watching a well coordinated and agile athlete play first base. Too often has this position been regarded lightly from a defensive standpoint. The saying that "anyone can play first" is not true on a championship caliber team. The first baseman may not be the most efficient fielder in the infield, but he must have quick hands and be able to handle all kinds of thrown balls. The player who aspires to become a top-notch first baseman must spend many hours working on his defensive play.

The left-handed first baseman has an advantage over the right-handed one in throws to second and third, on balls hit toward second, and in receiving throws from the pitcher and making the tag. The right-handed first baseman has the advantage on balls hit down the line, in tossing the ball to the pitcher covering first base, and on pickoff plays from the catcher. These advantages are so *slight* that they are almost meaningless.

Height is a definite asset. A tall man can reach farther and give the other fielders a better target. This does not mean that the tallest player should automatically be installed at first. A smaller player can compensate for his lack of height with speed and quickness.

Though a good arm is desirable, it need not be as strong as the other arms in the infield. Excellent footwork is particularly important for handling inaccurate throws and shifting properly. Also essential is the ability to size up situations and to make the basic throws effectively. All these techniques can be mastered through hard and constant practice. The other infielders must have complete confidence in the first baseman's ability to handle all balls thrown at him. Otherwise, they may become too cautious and begin aiming their throws.

Good hands are a natural physical attribute. Although everyone can improve, it is doubtful that a player can become an outstanding defensive first baseman without this quality. The importance of good hands lies in the fact that they are indispensable to maximum effectiveness in catching the many and varied throws that a first baseman is called on to handle in the course of a ball game. When he has acquired the knack of digging low throws out of the dirt and has learned the correct tactical maneuvers, he will have the respect of all his teammates.

RECEIVING THROWS

On a play to first, the first baseman runs directly to the base as soon as the ball is hit. Since he must get there in time to be in position, he must not play so far from the base that it will take an extra effort to be there before the throw.

Upon reaching the base, he uses various techniques. His first responsibility is to find the base and maintain complete body balance. Usually, a first baseman locates the base with his heel, and then faces the thrower, placing his feet a few inches in front of the base, approximately a base-width apart (Fig. 9-1).

To achieve the maximum stretch, he must line up his body directly with the thrower. *He should not shift until the throw is on the way.* This is a split-second move that is fundamental to good defensive play. A young player frequently errs by placing one foot on the base and reaching before the fielder releases the ball. This position ties him up and prevents his shifting.

The first baseman should learn all he possibly can about the abilities of the other infielders. He should know, for instance, if a fielder has a strong or a weak arm, and whether his throws take off or sink.

Figure 9-1

When receiving a throw from his right, the right-handed first baseman places his left foot against the outfield side of the base, and then steps for the catch with his right foot toward the throw (Fig. 9-2). However, some prefer crossing over with the left foot and backhanding the ball. On a wild throw, the main objective is to stop the ball and then if possible to tag the base.

On a throw to his left, the first baseman places his right foot against the inside corner of the base and steps toward the throw with his left foot (Fig. 9-3). If the throw is wide, he leaves the bag for the catch, then tags the runner coming down the line—making sure not to interfere with him.

Figure 9-2

When the ball is thrown directly at him, the right-handed first baseman places his right foot on the second-base side of the base and faces the thrower (Fig. 9-4). The reverse is true for the left-handed first baseman. On a close play he must stretch as far as possible in order to make the catch as quickly as possible. The long stretch often spells the difference between an "out" or "safe" call.

As soon as he catches the ball, he should pull his contact foot off the base. On throws received below his waist, the *palm* of his glove points upward (Fig. 9-4). On throws above his waist, the *fingers* of his glove point upward as shown in Figure 9-3.

Some coaches prefer that the first baseman always tag the base with the same foot. They feel it involves less teaching and that it does not reduce fielding efficiency. It is the author's opinion that the "one-footed" theory should be taught only if a player cannot master shifting his feet. If he can learn to shift his feet, he is facing the majority of the balls thrown to him.

Throws in the dirt should be fielded as close as possible to the point of contact. If the baseman cannot take the throw on the short hop, he should try to block it with his body. Some throws can be taken on the long hop. The art of stopping the low throw can be improved through constant practice.

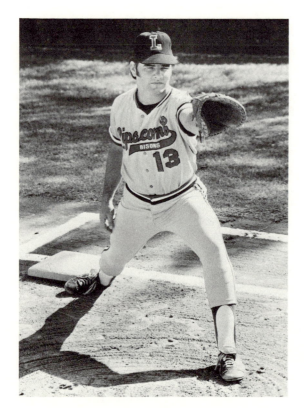

Figure 9-3

On high throws directly over the base, the baseman may have to leap straight up to make the catch. He should try to come down on the infield side of the base on such plays. If the throw is beyond his reach, he will have to leave the bag and then try for the out.

On a throw from the home-plate area, the first baseman places his right foot on the home-plate side of the base and extends his glove toward the thrower as a target (Fig. 9-5).

On a throw to the foul-line side of first, the baseman steps across the base into foul territory with his left foot and places his right (contact) foot on the foul-line side of the base (Fig. 9-6). As soon as he makes the catch, he pivots toward the infield for a possible play elsewhere.

Figure 9-4

FIELDING GROUNDERS

The first baseman's deployment is dictated by his fielding ability and the game situation. He must know the hitters in order to play them properly, and he must also be aware of the score, the outs, the inning, the count, and the ability of the base runners.

He must consider also both his and the second baseman's ground-covering ability, and know how the second baseman deploys for the various hitters. This will enable him to decide how far to play from the base. *Note:* The second baseman should always call for any grounder which he believes he can handle that is between himself and the first baseman.

Figure 9-5

Since aggressiveness is a great asset to any infielder, the championship first baseman must defy the ball, as it were. He must learn to charge the ball quickly, whenever possible, and to field it on a favorable bounce. If this is impossible, he must learn to short-hop it.

Since the ball does not always take a true bounce, the first baseman must carry his hands below the expected height of the bounce, as he can raise his hands more quickly than he can lower them. It is also important that he not pull his hands away from the ball too quickly, since this tendency produces many unnecessary errors.

The first baseman has a decided advantage over the other infielders in that he has fewer throws to make after fielding a grounder and rarely has to hurry a long throw.

Figure 9-6

Before every pitch, he must evaluate the situation in order to know what action to take on any batted ball. Thorough preparation will prevent many costly mistakes.

TEAMING WITH THE PITCHER

Since the pitcher covers first on all balls hit to the left of the mound, the first baseman, upon fielding the ball, must decide if he can make the putout unassisted. If he can, he should immediately wave the pitcher off. He should then hustle to first, step on the infield side of the base, and turn immediately toward the infield to avoid colliding with the runner.

When fielding the ball close to the foul line, however, he

may have to run across the base into foul territory. If there are runners on base, he should then turn immediately toward the infield, ready to make another play.

If he cannot make the putout unassisted, he must throw to the pitcher, who is covering. As soon as he fields the ball, he should pull his glove hand away and deliver the ball to the pitcher.

If he is close to the base, he should step toward the pitcher and toss the ball underhanded (Fig. 9-7). The throw should reach the pitcher chest-high, two or three steps from the base, so that he can easily make the catch and tag the base.

Figure 9-7

One of the first baseman's toughest plays occurs when he is uncertain whether the pitcher will be able to field a ground ball. He must not assume that the pitcher will field it. He must start for the ball, evaluate the situation, and, if he can make the play, call for it and throw to the pitcher covering first base. If the pitcher can make the play, he should call for the ball and continue on to first base, making the putout unassisted. This procedure eliminates the pressure decision the first baseman must often make concerning who is fielding the ball and covering first base.

Sometimes the first baseman will bobble the ball, or the ball will be hit so slowly that the pitcher can reach the base before the first baseman is ready to throw. In this case the pitcher should stop, put one foot on the base, and step toward the thrower with the other foot. The first baseman should then throw overhand directly to the base.

HOLDING A BASE RUNNER ON BASE

In holding a runner on, the first baseman faces the pitcher with his right foot along the home-plate side of the base, his toes even with the corner, his left foot on the first baseline, and his glove about three feet from the ground, extended toward the pitcher (Fig. 9-8).

Figure 9-8

In this position he can take a throw just in front of the base and merely drop his glove to the ground to complete the tag. He lets the runner come to him; he does not go after the runner. If the runner does not slide, the first baseman tries to touch the tagging foot.

If the runner on first is not likely to steal, the first baseman sometimes moves off the base behind the runner to prevent the ball from being hit down the line (Fig. 9-9). When the pitch is delivered, he may back up a step or two from this position.

Figure 9-9

Whenever the first baseman decides to change positions, he should inform the pitcher accordingly to prevent a balk or a wild throw.

On a bunt situation with runners on first and second, the first baseman plays in front of the runner, usually on the edge of the grass. He also plays in close on an anticipated squeeze play.

THROWING

As noted earlier, the first baseman need not have as strong an arm as the other infielders. His throwing ability is important, however, and if he has a strong arm, so much the better.

The first baseman must know what type of throw to use in every situation. The throw to second is generally made overhand because it has more carry and is more nearly accurate. When the throw must be made quickly, however, the sidearm delivery is used. If the ball is fielded on the infield grass, the throw should be made to the infield side of second; if it is fielded behind the baseline, the throw should be to the outfield side.

The first baseman's throws to the plate are usually short, since they are most likely made when the infield is playing in. He must get the throw off quickly and accurately. The way to develop quick and accurate throwing is to concentrate on making *every* practice throw a perfect one.

CUTOFF PLAYS

Almost all the other first-baseman throws stem from cutoff plays. The number of cutoff plays involving him will depend largely on the system employed by the coach.

In most cutoff systems, the first baseman serves as the "cut" man on all throws to the plate except on singles to left field. This method seems to provide the most nearly complete coverage for all bases. For simplicity, some coaches use the first baseman as the cutoff man on *all* throws to the plate.

There are advantages to both systems, but for thorough coverage of all bases on a single, the third baseman is used on any ball hit to left. The latter setup also enables the defense to trap the batter as he rounds first. This will not provide coverage at first on singles to right and center fields on which the second baseman cannot cover. But the outfielders, by keeping their throws low, can prevent the runners from advancing.

The first baseman should hold his hands high above his head as a target whenever he is in the cutoff position so that the outfielders will be able to see him more easily.

DEFENSING THE BUNT

On an anticipated bunt with a runner on first, the first baseman charges toward the plate as the pitcher starts his delivery. This run should not be straight down the line; the first two steps should be taken at a 45° angle into the infield. Hence, if the ball is bunted hard and to the first baseman's right, he is in position to field it and go for the force play at second. If the ball is bunted in front of him, he fields it and throws to the base called by the catcher.

If the first baseman knows he cannot get the batter on a slow bunt down the line, he should permit the ball to roll if there is a chance that it may go foul. With a runner on, the first baseman must be alert to prevent his taking an extra base. On a bunt in foul territory close to the line, the first baseman should touch it as quickly as possible to keep it from rolling fair.

Whenever possible, the first baseman should cover first on all bunts toward third. Whenever the catcher must cover third, the first baseman should be alert to cover the plate. Whenever the first baseman is unable to get back to cover first, the second baseman assumes this duty.

POINTS TO REMEMBER

The first baseman should:

1. Get to the base as quickly as possible to shift right or left for the throw.
2. Present a target to the inside of the base whenever the catcher, pitcher, or third baseman is throwing from the plate area.
3. Carry his hands low in fielding grounders.
4. *Always expect a bad throw.* Good throws are easy to catch.
5. Field grounders in front of his body.
6. Leave the base to catch extra-wide throws.
7. Team with the pitcher, if necessary, to make the putout.
8. Hold the runner close on an anticipated steal.
9. When charging a bunt with a runner on first, take the first two steps at a 45° angle into the infield.
10. On a bunt toward third, cover first, if possible, and, after getting the ball, rush toward any runner caught between bases.
11. On a dropped third strike, present a target in foul territory, as the ball will usually go behind the catcher.
12. Let the catcher know when a runner is stealing.

13. Cover the area up to the pitcher's mound on any bunt attempt to advance a runner from second to third.

14. Back up the second baseman on all throws from left field.

15. Use two hands in fielding, whenever possible.

16. On a ground ball or throw to the plate side of first with a runner on third, run the batter-runner back toward the plate if he pulls up, to help prevent the runner from scoring.

17. Step toward second base in making a throw for a force-out.

18. Throw to the infield side of second base for a force-out when the ball has been fielded on the infield grass.

19. Work a pitchout with the catcher if the runner can be caught off first.

20. Make no move to shift feet until the ball is in flight to him.

10

AGGRESSIVE
THIRD-BASE PLAY

Playing third base requires sharp reflexes and quick thinking. Physical strength and a strong throwing arm are very
important to the third baseman. He should be physically strong
so that he can block hard-hit balls with his body, if necessary;
and he must have a strong, accurate arm, since it is a significant
distance across the diamond. He must be able to throw from any
position in which he fields the ball. Running speed is not essential, but quick reactions, a sure pair of hands, and the ability to
handle the ball quickly are important. He is called upon to move
only short distances to field batted balls, but quickness is necessary for successful performance. A third baseman must be able
to charge in fast on slowly-hit and bunted balls.

The third baseman must be aggressive and mentally tough.
His fielding position often will bring him close to the batter,
where he will be required to field sharply hit ground balls.
Maintaining correct body position in this situation is not easy.
The natural reaction is to pull away from such a ball; however,
the third baseman must learn to stay in proper position. This is
the nucleus of aggressive third-base play.

TECHNIQUES OF THIRD-BASE PLAY

The third baseman's position probably requires more versatility than any other fielding position. Mental alertness to each possible play situation helps to make an aggressive third baseman. When the bases are unoccupied with fewer than two outs, he should anticipate a possible bunt for a base hit. If expecting a bunt, he should position himself anywhere from even with third base to five feet ahead of the baseline between second and third bases, depending on his knowledge of the batter.

One of the mistakes made most often by a young third baseman is the assumption that a ground ball is not his. But he should play any ground ball that he can reach cleanly on either side of him.

The third baseman's normal position for a batter who does not bunt is approximately ten to fifteen feet from the foul line and about three or four yards behind the base. If the batter is a "pull hitter," the third baseman should move closer to the foul line.

If a team is ahead by a run going into late innings, most coaches prefer that their third baseman play a little closer to the foul line in order to guard against an extra-base hit. It is not a good idea for him to play close to the line consistently. More balls are hit into the area between shortstop and third base than are hit down the line.

A third baseman who plays well off the line is a tremendous help to the shortstop. The ball hit to his right is one of the hardest plays the shortstop must make. If he can move toward second base, he can reach balls hit up the middle of the diamond.

FIELDING GROUND BALLS

The fielding stance of the third baseman is wider and lower than that of any fielder (Fig. 10-1). By spreading his feet farther apart, he lowers his center of mass and increases his stability. He bends at the waist and extends his arms down in front of his body. This extra stability enables him to stay with the sharp-hit ground ball and to move quickly in either of three directions.

Figure 10-1

The fact that this stance is low helps the third baseman when he does not have time to move down from a more upright position to field batted balls. This is particularly true in the case of the sharply hit ground ball. Also, from this position the third baseman will get a better angle on the ball and can follow it more readily. Just as the ball is being delivered by the pitcher, he should take a half step so he will be moving slowly forward when the ball is hit. It is important that the third baseman expects every ball to be hit to him and that he knows what to do when he fields it.

The third baseman advances as fast as possible on all slowly hit and bunted balls which he attempts to handle. He fields the ball in front of his right foot, as his left foot comes down on the ground (Fig. 10-2). The ball should be fielded with both hands whenever possible. Some college players can make the bare-hand scoop and underhand throw, but most coaches think this play is for professionals.

   If the ball is bunted or hit slowly close to the third baseline and is foul, it should be touched immediately. If the ball is fair, and the batter-runner cannot be thrown out, it should be permitted to roll, since there is a chance it will roll foul. However, if a runner is on base and will be able to advance while the ball is rolling, it should be picked up to keep the base runner from advancing.

Figure 10-2

   When first base is occupied and the third baseman fields a ground ball hit to his left, the throw should be to second base, provided he has time to make the play. This is a shorter throw than to first base, and he has his body moving in that direction.

   When second base is occupied and there are fewer than two

outs, the third baseman should "look the runner back" at second base after he fields a hard-hit ground ball. This forces the runner to stay closer to the base. The same should be done to a runner on third base. He will still have time to throw to first.

If there are runners on first and third base, no outs, and a close score, on a ball hit hard to the third baseman, he takes a quick look at the runner on third base. If he attempts to score, the throw is made immediately to the plate. If he does not break when the ball is hit, the third baseman makes his play to second base. Frequently, with one out the play goes to second for the double play from second to first. This strategy is used when the first and third baseman are playing in and when the shortstop and second baseman are playing back. With several runs ahead and fewer than two outs, the throw should go to second base for the double play, which lessens the chances of a big inning. In high school, such a play usually would be made to first base.

If second and third bases are occupied, with one out and a close score, most teams will attempt to have both runners advance on a ground ball to the third baseman. The play then is made to the catcher. With no outs, some teams will not attempt to advance unless the ball is hit slowly to the third baseman. In this situation he must decide if he has a play at home plate.

When third base is occupied, the third baseman must assume the same defensive position that he would if the runner were not there, but he should never ignore the runner.

When the third baseman has a play at the plate, he should throw the ball to the catcher as quickly as possible. Then he should break over and down the baseline for a possible rundown, if the runner stops and attempts to return to third base. The catcher can make a quick throw to the third baseman who can tag the runner retreating to third base. If the runner from second base has advanced to third, and the runner on third makes it back, the runner from second should be tagged. The runner who first occupied the base is entitled to it. To avoid confusion, however, both runners should be tagged.

SACRIFICE BUNT

When the sacrifice bunt is anticipated by the third baseman, he should watch the batter very closely; if the batter shifts the bat forward to bunt, he should charge toward home plate. If the batter draws his bat back, the third baseman should stop abruptly, anticipating a swing.

The position of the third baseman before he charges home plate is about five feet wide of third base and on the edge of the infield grass. From this position, he will go straight in on the ball when he fields it. If someone else fields the bunt, the third baseman should return immediately to third base.

When first and second bases are occupied and a bunt is expected, the third baseman assumes a position not more than five steps from third base. The pitcher covers the third-base side of the diamond by moving directly toward the foul line, while the third baseman stays close to the base for a possible force-out. The third baseman must be alert to field a ball bunted so hard that the pitcher cannot handle it. In this situation he should field the ball and make his throw to first base. If the batter attempts to hit, the third baseman breaks several steps to the left of his base, prepared to field a ball hit in his area.

When a runner is on second, the third baseman must be careful not to move from his position too quickly, leaving the base unprotected against a steal. Some teams will fake a bunt and steal in this situation. With two strikes on the batter, the third baseman usually can return to his normal position, depending on the batter. Some poor hitters may attempt a sacrifice bunt with two strikes on them.

HANDLING POP FLIES

The third baseman should take all fly balls between third base and home plate. He is in a much better position to catch fly balls in this area, and he should "run the catcher off" by calling loud and clear for the ball. The third baseman and the first baseman must also field pop flies in the area of the mound, since this is a difficult play for the pitcher.

The shortstop is in better position to handle pop flies behind third base and should call for the ball, so the third baseman will know he can make the play.

The third baseman covers third when second base is occupied and a fly ball is hit which he himself does not attempt to field. He does the same with third base occupied except when the catcher fields a fly ball, and the pitcher or first baseman leaves home plate uncovered. In this case, the third baseman covers home and the shortstop covers third base.

THROWING

The third baseman should throw overhanded to first base whenever possible. An overhand throw is generally faster and certainly more likely to be accurate. A ball thrown sidearm has a tendency to sail away and down. It is recommended that young players practice fielding ground balls and bringing themselves into a position immediately to throw overhanded.

In throwing, the grip of the baseball is very important to get maximum carry on it and to eliminate the possibility of its sailing. It should be gripped with the tips of the first two fingers and the thumb across the seams. Most major league third basemen favor gripping the ball across the seams. As the arm is brought back for the throw, the player can switch his fingers to the correct position without looking at the ball. Because of the variety of plays the third baseman has to handle, he must be proficient in throwing sidearm and underhand, as well as overhand.

The throw to second base to start a double play is of the utmost importance. The ball must reach the second baseman chest high and directly over the base. The third baseman should use a semi-crouch position and throw overhand to the base, if he must hurry his throw (Fig. 10-3). If the ball reaches him before the second baseman has time to get into position for the play, he can stand up and time his overhand throw to reach the base as the second baseman arrives. In some situations he will be forced to throw underhand or sidearm to the second baseman because of the speed of the ball and the position in which he finds himself.

If the ball is hit near the base with first and second occupied, the third baseman should touch third and throw to first for the double play. When the bases are loaded, the third baseman should go home with the ball for the force-out, and the

catcher can go to first for the double play. In professional baseball the play usually is made at second base to execute the double play, but in amateur baseball it usually is best to be sure the
runner does not score. Again, if the ball is hit near the base, the
third baseman should touch the base and go home with the ball,
letting the catcher know the force is off at the plate, and the
runner must be tagged.

Figure 10-3

RECEIVING THROWS

The third baseman should straddle the base, facing the direction from which the throw is coming, with his feet several
inches behind the front edge. If the throw is wide, he is in good
position to go to either side of the base to make the catch.

When the throw comes from the catcher on an attempted steal, the third baseman should straddle the back part of the base, with his body turned slightly toward the catcher. This leaves the base open for the runner and avoids the possibility of a collision with the third baseman. As he catches the ball, he makes the tag by turning left slightly and facing the runner. If the throw is wide, he is in good position to go to either side to make the catch. If he must leave the base to catch the ball, he does so.

When there is a runner on second base and third base is open, the third baseman should develop the habit of taking a step toward third base after the ball passes the batter. He should glance at the runner while he is taking this step. If this is done, he will always be in position to cover the base on an attempted steal.

If a runner is leading off third base, his lead normally is in foul territory; therefore, the catcher must throw to the second-base side of third base for a pickoff play. If the throw is accurate, there is little danger of the runner's being hit. As the third baseman catches the ball, he should step across the base with his right foot, facing the runner as he makes the tag.

On a force-out, when the third baseman receives a throw he should place his right foot on the corner of the base closest to the pitcher's mound and stretch forward with his left foot in the direction of the throw (Fig. 10-4).

Basically, there are two ways of tagging a base runner. One way is to bring the glove down in front of the base and then look for the runner's foot, tagging it with the back of the glove. It is important here that the infielder does not allow the runner to knock the ball out of his glove hand. Some infielders will smother the ball with both hands to prevent this. In this situation, the glove should be held a few inches away from the base so there is room to absorb the contact of the runner's foot.

The second way to tag a base runner is by sweeping the ball across the line of his slide. In receiving the throw, the third baseman sweeps the ball in an arc down across his foot and up again. If he has to wait, he does not plant his glove but holds it cocked to one side and times his sweep. When the base runner slides, he snaps the glove hand down and across his foot.

Figure 10-4

CUTOFF DUTIES

On base hits or fly balls to left field, the third baseman acts as the cutoff man for throws to the plate. He should place himself approximately sixty feet from home plate and in line with the outfielder. Some coaches prefer the cutoff position to be a little deeper, so that the third baseman can move toward the ball in order to make any necessary adjustments. When he reaches this position, he should raise both arms into the air, so the outfielder can easily locate the cutoff man (Fig. 10-5). If the throw is wide or late, the catcher instructs the third baseman to cut off the throw and alerts him for a possible play on the batter runner. When the third baseman becomes the cutoff man, the shortstop covers third base. Most coaches agree that the throw from the outfield should be caught on the fly by the cutoff man.

Figure 10-5

TACTICAL SUMMARY

The outstanding third baseman is, of necessity, an aggressive ball player. He is eager for the ball to be hit to him. The basic philosophy of the position is to take any ball that he can get. To get the jump on the ball, the third baseman should watch the hitter, not the pitcher.

When there is a runner on second base, the third baseman should develop the habit of taking a step toward third after the ball passes the batter, so as to be in position to cover the base on a steal. He should not be drawn in too quickly on fake bunts, leaving the base open for the steal.

He should be alert for possible throws from the catcher for a pickoff. With many ball clubs the throw is automatic on a missed swing by the batter.

When first base is occupied and a base hit goes to the outfield, the third baseman covers his base. If it is to right field and the base runner continues on to third base, the third baseman should give instructions to the shortstop to cut off the throw if it is wide or late.

The third baseman should check the runners rounding the base on the way home and the men tagging up to score after a fly ball is caught. Alertness on such plays can save a team runs and in some instances a ball game.

POINTS TO REMEMBER

Some of the following "Points to Remember" are basic rules for an aggressive third baseman:

1. Check the terrain around third base before the game starts.

2. Always watch the hitter, not the pitcher, when the pitch is being delivered to the batter. This makes a better jump on the ball possible and aids in early detection of a bunt.

3. With two outs, guard the foul line in an effort to prevent an extra base hit.

4. When any base is occupied, back up throws from the first baseman to the pitcher.

5. Block hard-hit balls, because the batter may very often be thrown out at first base even through the ball is not fielded cleanly.

6. Attempt to field any ball to your left, because this position usually is a difficult chance for the shortstop.

7. Listen for the catcher's voice if in doubt as to where to make a throw.

8. Think ahead on every play, and study the opposing hitters.

9. Give way to the shortstop on fly balls back of third base.

10. When the bases are loaded, make the double play home to first.

11. Be alert for a squeeze play with third occupied and fewer than two outs in a close ball game.

12. **Permit** slow-hit balls along the foul line to roll when the **batter** cannot be retired at first.

13. **Field** bunts and slow-hit balls with two hands, if possible.

14. Cover third base unless you are required to perform some other duty on defense.

15. With runners on first and second, go for the double play by way of second, unless the ball is hit close to the base.

16. Be alert for a fake bunt with second base occupied. This may be a planned play to help the runner steal third.

17. Take the cutoff position for throws to the plate after a single to left field with a runner in scoring position.

18. Never back up on balls hit directly at you, since this in effect allows the ball to play you.

19. Watch each runner rounding the base on his way home, and check the men tagging up to score after a fly ball is caught. Call for an appeal play if the runner misses the base or leaves too soon on a fly ball.

20. Call "Cut" to the shortstop if a throw to third base is wide or if the runner cannot be retired. No call means, "Let the ball go."

11

COACHING CHAMPIONSHIP
KEYSTONE STRATEGY

Very few teams have achieved championship heights without a smooth-working, dependable keystone combination. The
second baseman and the shortstop form the heart of the defense.
They are called upon to handle all sorts of vital plays, and they
must learn to work together. The key to their success is in direct
proportion to the extent that they work together harmoniously.
Innate ability tempered by constant practice is extremely perti-
nent to the ultimate success of the keystone combination in
fulfilling its role as the heart of the team. You, as the coach, will
have to spend a great deal of time developing them.

CHAMPIONSHIP SECOND BASE PLAY

When you realize that one of the keys to championship
baseball is the double play, and that the second baseman is in
more double plays than anyone else, you must realize that this is
a very important position. The second baseman must be able to
make the double play consistently if a team is to play championship baseball. This is the reason the shortstop and second base-

man must practice making this play over and over, until they know each other's every move.

Qualifications. This position does not require any special size, but it does demand a strong arm and excellent speed. Since the second baseman must serve as the pivot man on many double plays, he must have agility, quick mental reactions, and the ability to throw from any position. No other player on the team will make as many different types of throws as a good second baseman. Quickness is a second baseman's greatest asset.

Making the Double Play. The second baseman may shift his feet several ways at second base to catch the ball for a force-out and throw to first base. As soon as the ball is hit, he must move to the base as quickly as possible and assume a set position. This give the shortstop a stationary target and enables the second baseman to receive the throw and to shift in any direction.

If he cannot get to the base under control, he is playing too far away from it. The second baseman must cheat in toward the plate and a couple of steps closer to the base. It is important to be in proper position. The pivot should *not* be made on the run—the feet should be set for the throw to first. One of the simplest pivots to teach, and a very effective way to evade the base runner, is for the second baseman to step on the base with his left foot (Fig. 11-1), and then into the diamond with his right foot (Fig. 11-2) to make the throw (Fig. 11-3).

If the feeding throw is accurate and the runner is far enough away, the baseman can step on the base with his right foot just as he catches the ball, and then step toward first base with his left foot for the throw.

If the runner is close and on the infield side of the baseline, the second baseman may place his left foot on the outfield side of second base to make the catch (Fig. 11-4), then push back to his right foot, and step toward first with his left foot to complete the throw (Fig. 11-5).

If the throw to second goes to the second baseman's right, he steps on the left field side of the base with his left foot and out with his right foot to make the catch. He then shifts his weight to the right foot and steps toward first with the left for the throw.

If the throw is to the second baseman's left, he places his

Figure 11-1

right foot on the home-plate corner of the base and steps out to his left with his left foot for the catch. If the runner is close, the baseman must step forward with the right foot after the catch, out of the way of the runner, and then toward first with the left foot for his throw.

If the second baseman can get to the base quickly enough, he may straddle it (Fig. 11-6). Then, if the throw is accurate, he can step toward first with his left foot and drag his right toe against the left-field side of the base for the throw (Fig. 11-7).

CHAMPIONSHIP FIELDING AND THROWING

The key points in fielding ground balls are to stay low, watch the ball, and be relaxed. The ball is fielded with the hands

Figure 11-2

out in front, and they must be soft, so it can be caught properly. The secret of being a successful fielder is to keep the eyes on the ball and to be sure not to raise the head too soon.

The infielder should charge most ground balls that are hit in his direction. The hard hit ball will not require him to charge forward, but he should be ready on each pitch to move toward the batter.

The second baseman must learn to play the hitter properly, just as all other players on the field. The knowledge of where the batter hits the ball and how fast he runs determines where the field should normally play. This can be a major asset to him. The more information he has about a particular hitter and the pitcher on the mound, the better he will be able to play his position. Experienced infielders get excellent jumps on ground

Figure 11-3

balls because they know what pitch is being thrown and the type of hitter at the plate.

The second baseman's throw is more of a snap overhand than throws of other infielders and outfielders. This mainly is due to his getting rid of the ball from the position in which he fields it. Many times he will not be able to straighten up for the throw and step toward the base with the left foot. On many occasions he will be required to get rid of the ball very quickly. The secret to the quick release when throwing is to catch it with two hands out in front of the body, and, with a continuous motion, bring both hands back into a throwing position. As the hands go back to throw, the fielder has a chance to grip the ball securely and get into position to throw. You should warn all fielders to catch the ball before they try to throw. Many times the

Figure 11-4

infielders will try to throw before they have caught the ball.

Whenever the second baseman is called upon to throw to second for a force-out, he should try to make his footwork as simple as possible. After fielding a ground ball to his left, he should pivot to his right on his left foot, swing the right foot behind the left, and then step out with the left foot toward second to complete the throw.

If he can come to a full stop and set himself, he should pivot on his right foot and step toward second with his left for the throw. He should not stand upright, but should remain in a semi-squat for the pivot. As he throws, he may rise slightly, but the faster he must make the play, the less he should raise his body.

After fielding a grounder while moving toward second, the baseman should immediately pull his gloved hand away so that the shortstop can see the ball. Then, using only the forearm and

Figure 11-5

wrist, he can toss the ball underhand to the shortstop (Fig. 11-8).

If only a step or two from the base, the baseman should step on it for the force-out, and then make the throw to first himself. This action can be performed quickly and will eliminate the chance of an error on a toss. Whenever the baseman can make the play, he should call, "I've got it!" to prevent the shortstop from interfering with him.

Upon fielding a ground ball hit directly to him, the baseman should pivot to the right on the balls of both feet, so that the toes point toward second, and then make the throw (Fig. 11-9). This usually is a short, overhand snap from a squat. For a longer throw, the baseman will have to use more body, arm, and leg power. On a ground ball fielded directly behind second, the baseman may backhand it to the shortstop from the gloved hand. This can be done only, of course, from a short distance.

Figure 11-6

Playing a Bunt. The second baseman sets up close to first so that he can cover first in the event the first baseman is unable to do so. Unless he has a pickoff play with the catcher, the second baseman should hold this position until the ball is bunted or until the pitch passes the batter. Leaving too soon will open a hole in the defense. To avoid this, the second baseman can advance toward the plate until the ball is bunted. Such an advance also shortens the distance to first.

Upon reaching first, the baseman should place his left foot on the second-base side of the base and his right foot into the diamond, giving the fielder a good target. As soon as he makes the putout, he should turn into the diamond, alert for a possible play at third. Whenever the first baseman covers for the throw, the second baseman should back him up.

Figure 11-7

When a bunt is expected with men on first and second, the second baseman should always cover first, since the first baseman will be playing in for a possible force at third. In this situation, the second baseman should (after taking the throw) be alert for a possible play at the plate. With a runner on second only, the play is made the same as with a runner on first.

Balls to the Outfield. The second baseman covers second on all balls hit to left until he is certain the shortstop can cover. He then backs up the throw from the outfielder.

The second baseman generally takes all relays on balls to right field. As the ball is hit, he swings toward second, watching the outfielder making the play. If the ball is fielded cleanly, he receives the throw from the fielder. If the throw is wide, he runs

Figure 11-8

toward it, acting as cutoff man, while the shortstop comes in to cover.

The second baseman, hence, covers second on all hits to right except those past the rightfielder. On open fields, such hits usually will be good for at least three bases; so the second baseman must go out and take the relay throw to the plate. When getting to his relay position in the outfield, he should raise both hands above his head. After the throw has been made from the outfielder, the second baseman should take the throw with his body turned toward the left. He steps forward with his right foot in the direction of the throw. This half turn of his body toward the infield enables him to make his throw more quickly. Failure to use this maneuver just wastes valuable time.

When first base is occupied, the second baseman should

Figure 11-9

cover second on any single to right field that is fielded cleanly.
The throw will go to third base. If it is wide or too late to catch
the runner attempting to reach third, the shortstop will cut it off
and possibly make a play on the batter-runner. Should the lead
runner make a long turn at second, the second baseman will be
in position for a play from the shortstop.

Many teams use the double cutoff. This will send the second
baseman or shortstop out behind the other player in case of a bad
throw. The outfielder should throw to the first man who comes
out for the throw. The second man is about thirty feet behind as
a backup. If the throw is too high or too low, the second man
takes it.

The second baseman and shortstop should work together on
giving the other instructions on where to throw the ball when

they are in the relay position. Quickness in this situation is very important, and the information on where to throw must be received by the relay man before he gets the ball.

Fly Balls in the Infield. When the first baseman fields a foul or fair fly ball with a man on first, the second baseman must cover first. This also holds true on a fair fly ball with no one on first.

If the second baseman fields a fly ball back of him with a man on base, he should immediately run toward the infield to prevent the runner from attempting to advance. This is particularly true with third base occupied.

When the shortstop fields a fly ball, the second baseman covers second. If the shortstop and third baseman go after a fly ball with a man on second, the second baseman covers third, unless the pitcher does so.

Working with the First Baseman. The second baseman should try for any slow- or medium-hit ground ball to his left. As soon as he is sure he can make the play, he should call to the first baseman, running him back to first for the throw. The second baseman is in better position to make the play, since he is moving in the direction of his throw.

When the ball is fielded in the area of the plate with the first baseman covering his base, the second baseman backs up the throw. He also backs up second whenever the shortstop covers the base on a throw from the plate area.

On grounders to his right, the second baseman should try to get in front of the ball, stopping squarely in front of it and bracing on his right leg. The braced leg furnishes a firm support for the subsequent throw.

CHAMPIONSHIP SHORTSTOP PLAY

Qualifications. The shortstop is a key man in the infield. He should have a sure pair of hands, a strong arm, and quickness. He must be able to throw accurately from a variety of positions, to charge slow-hit ground balls, and to move right or left for the hard ground balls. Baseball sense and anticipation are also valuable assets; height, though not essential, is an advantage. The shortstop is often a team leader, the type of player who will take charge in the infield. Few teams have risen to championship heights without a smooth-working shortstop.

Making the Double Play. As soon as the ball is hit, the shortstop should get to the base as quickly as possible and assume a set position for the throw. As emphasized at second base, the pivot should not be made on the run, if possible.

The simplest and most popular pivot presents itself when the throw is received a step to the outfield side of the base. The right foot is placed on the right-field side of the base as he steps out with his left foot for the catch (Fig. 11-10). He then brings his right foot behind the left and steps toward first with his left for the throw (Fig. 11-11). These steps will carry him well away from the runner.

If the throw is to his right, the shortstop places his left foot on the third-base side of the base and steps out with his right to receive the throw (Fig. 11-12). He then pivots on his right foot and steps into the diamond with his left foot for the throw (Fig. 11-13).

When time permits, the shortstop may straddle the base and make his throw in front of the slider. As he receives the ball, he places his left foot on the right-field side of the base, then brings his right foot over the base, and steps out with his left for the throw. If the runner is close, the step with the left foot should be away from him.

Many experts consider the leap-flip as the fastest way to make the double play, although it is the hardest to learn. The shortstop hits the base with his right foot and makes a flat flip throw to first, jumping in the air to avoid the runner. Most amateur shortstops make inaccurate throws to first base using this method because of throwing off-balance.

The throw to the shortstop from the catcher or pitcher should be made to the base, chest high. If he is moving, it should be slightly toward the third-base side. The shortstop usually will take his throw on the run and, as he catches the ball, steps on the base.

If he steps on the base with his right foot, he must use it as a pivot in stepping out with his left foot for the throw. If he steps on the base with his left foot as he makes the catch, he should

Figure 11-10

step toward first with his right foot and then with his left for the throw. The step should be away from the runner (toward the inside of the diamond) if the play is close.

Championship Throwing and Fielding. One of the most difficult problems facing young infielders is throwing properly. Many of them throw across their bodies, which makes them very inaccurate. They don't step in the direction they are throwing, which is the proper way. Many infielders do not grip the ball across the seams, which is the proper technique. The infielder should not throw a ball that will sink or rise. Proper throwing must be stressed by all coaches. The ball should not be gripped too tightly or too loosely, just snugly enough for control over it.

Upon fielding a ground ball with a double play in order, the shortstop ordinarily should not straighten up; he should throw

Figure 11-11

from the position in which he fields the ball. On a ground ball hit directly at him, he may take a short step with his left foot in the direction of his throw, at the same time pulling his gloved hand down and away as he makes a snap overhand throw (Fig. 11-14).

Sometimes he will be called upon to throw from a squat position, using only arm action. In this case, he would not take a step but would pivot left on the balls of his feet so that his toes point in the direction of his throw.

Upon fielding a ground ball to his left (close to the base), he should pull his gloved hand away from the ball to show it, and then toss underhand to second, using a wrist and forearm snap rather than a full-arm swing (Fig. 11-15).

If the shortstop is only a step or two from the base as he catches the ball, he should call, "I've got it!" and make the play

Figure 11-12

himself. The call is necessary to prevent the second baseman from coming into the base and interfering with the play.

On a ground ball to his right, the shortstop should move into position as quickly as possible, stopping squarely in front of the ball by bracing his right leg. He should throw immediately after fielding the ball, as he will rarely have time to straighten up. Usually, he will have to use a snap overhand or sidearm throw, depending on the position in which he fielded the ball. If he finds that a step with his left foot is necessary, he should make it short and in the direction of the throw.

The principles of fielding ground balls are the same for the shortstop as for the second baseman. He must keep his eyes on the ball and stay low. His glove should be close to the ground and his body in front of the ball. His eyes follow the ball into his

Figure 11-13

glove. The ball should be fielded with both hands if at all possible. If both hands are used, he will be able to throw more quickly. He will have much better control of the ball and will make fewer errors.

It is very important for the shortstop to charge all ground balls, if possible. It is better to charge a ball than to lay back or back up. If the shortstop lays back, more than likely he will field the ball between hops. Aggressiveness is a desirable trait in championship shortstop play.

The toughest play for the shortstop is going to his right. He must go for the ball very quickly, plant his right foot, and field the ball at the same time. The braced right leg gives a firm support as the fielder steps out with his left foot in the direction of the throw.

Figure 11-14

Playing the Bunt. With first occupied and a bunt anticipated, the shortstop should move closer to second (double-play
position) to facilitate his coverage.

With first and second occupied, no one out, the shortstop
holds the runner close to second for a possible force at third. He
should set up no more than two or three steps behind the base.
As the pitcher delivers, he should move over to cover his normal
position, unless the batter drops his bat for a bunt. With two
strikes on the batter, the shortstop should take his double-play
position.

Balls to the Outfield. On a single to right with no one on
base, the shortstop covers second until the second baseman
comes over to cover. He then backs up the throw to the base.

Figure 11-15

On a single to left, he covers the base if the ball is fielded cleanly. If the throw is wide, he leaves the base for the cutoff.

On a single to right with a man on first, the shortstop runs to a cutoff position for the throw to third. If the throw is made to second, he backs it up. On throws to third, the shortstop is given instructions by the third baseman. If the latter calls "Cut!" the shortstop looks for a play on the back runner—anticipating an attempted advance to second or a wide turn at first.

On a single to left with a man on first, the shortstop lines up with the throw to third, about 15 to 20 yards from the base. If the throw is wide, he cuts it off and looks for a possible play on the back runner.

When second or third is occupied, the shortstop covers third

on base hits and fly balls to the outfield, while the third baseman acts as the cutoff man.

The shortstop usually takes all relays on balls hit past the
left or center fielders. As the ball is hit, he swings toward second, watching the play. If the hit is a single that can be fielded
cleanly, he takes the throw from the outfielder.

If the ball passes the outfielder, he runs toward him, at the
same time listening for directions from the second baseman. He
hustles to a position in line with the outfielder's throw and the
base to which he will throw. He should be close enough to catch
the relay on the fly. After the throw has been made from the
outfielder, he should take the throw with his body turned toward
the left. This half turn of his body toward the infield enables him
to make his throw more quickly.

Fly Balls in the Infield. The shortstop covers second on all
fly balls taken by the second baseman, and third on all fly balls
taken by the third baseman. The shortstop should take most fly
balls hit directly behind the third baseman, as he is in better
position to handle the ball by not having to turn and run
backward.

On a fly ball back of him, with someone on base, the shortstop should, as soon as he catches the ball, run toward the infield
to prevent the runner from advancing. This is particularly true
with a man on third.

Charging Ground Balls. The shortstop should move in as
fast as possible on all ground balls coming his way to save time
and cut down the length of the throws. Playing a ball too slow is
a common fault among inexperienced shortstops.

With second occupied and fewer than two outs, the shortstop should, on a ground ball hit sharply to him or to his right,
glance at the runner and fake him back to the base before throwing to first. With two outs, the play is normally made to first.

If, with second base occupied, the shortstop fumbles a ball
and the runner advances, he should be alert for a possible play
at third; a quick throw can pick off any runner making a long
turn.

The shortstop covers second on all grounders hit to the first-base side of second and in the home-plate and pitcher's area, except when his position makes it impossible.

When the third baseman goes in for a slow roller with a man on first, the shortstop covers third, unless the catcher or pitcher gets there first.

Charging the Slow Roller. Another tough play for the shortstop is the slow roller. He must charge forward, field the ball, and throw to a base while on the move. If he waits for the slow roller to reach him, a fast runner will reach the base safely.

This play will require a strong, accurate underhand throw, which must be made very quickly. It is more successful when made with two hands, if at all possible. The bare, one-hand grab should be made as a last resort. The bare-hand pickup requires considerable skill.

If the ball has stopped rolling, the infielder should charge it from the left side and field it with the bare hand. In one motion, he picks the ball up and makes the throw.

If the shortstop has to approach the ball from the side, he should field it with the gloved hand in front of the left foot. If the face of the glove is open, the ball will roll into it, and the shortstop can throw to first base in one continuous move.

Tagging the Runners. A neglected area of teaching infield play has often been making the tag on a sliding runner. The safest tag is straddling the base with the glove on the ground in front of the bag and letting the runner slide into it. To make sure the sliding runner does not kick the ball out of the glove, the infielder should close the thumb over the glove. It also is wise to remove the glove from the tag position as soon as the sliding runner touches it.

On the sweep tag, the infielder stands with both feet behind the base and sweeps the ball across the line of the runner's slide. In receiving the throw, he sweeps the ball in an arc, down across the foot, and up again. If he has to wait for the runner, he should not place his glove in the runner's path with the ball exposed. This is an excellent way to have it kicked out of the glove. He should have the glove cocked to one side and should time his sweep as the runner slides.

POINTS TO REMEMBER

The keystone combination should:

1. Use mouth signals to decide who will cover second on some straight-away hitters.

2. Employ a verbal sign to inform the first and third baseman of a slow ball or change of pace.

3. Use a closed fist for a fastball, an open hand for a curve, and a wiggle of the fingers for a change-up in signaling pitches to the outfield.

4. Stretch for the force-out at second whenever the double play cannot be made, as well as when there are two outs.

5. Be alert to retrieve a catcher's errant throw to the pitcher.

6. Call "I have it!" if you can make the force-out at second unassisted, so that your teammate will not interfere with the play.

7. Call "Cut!" to the cutoff man if the throw to second is wide or if the runner cannot be retired. No call means not to intercept the ball.

8. Take a position approximately 100 to 150 feet from an outfielder when acting as a relay man. Spin toward the glove hand and throw to the base on a hop.

9. Stand just in front of second when handling the catcher's peg on a first-and-third steal. Break in to take the throw if the runner on third attempt to score, unless it is more important to catch the runner advancing from first.

10. Make long relay throws to third and home on a hop.

11. Practice the double-team pickoff play. The player designated to cover fakes the pickoff; then the other player breaks for the base.

12. Move in a step or two with a man on first to increase the chances for a double play.

13. Always make sure of the first out.

14. Take a step or two toward second after the ball has passed the batter with a runner on first. This prevents a delayed steal.

15. Position themselves for the hit-and-run with a runner on first and the pitcher behind the hitter.

16. Move two steps in with men on first and third and the count at 3-1 or 3-2; this is a double-steal situation.

17. Ignore the man on third unless he is the tying or winning run with men on first and third.

18. Always decide who will do what before the next play.

19. Use a quick snap throw, letter high, to the pivot man.

20. Get to the base quickly if you are the pivot man, and use any extra time to coordinate the pivot.

12

AGGRESSIVE
OUTFIELD PLAY

The outfielders are too often the most neglected players on the baseball team in terms of instruction and practice. Most coaches do not provide adequate drills for them, and many players perform for years without improving their skills. It is often said, "Anyone can play the outfield." Nothing is further from the truth than such a statement. There are two general weaknesses in this theory. First, an error by an outfielder is usually more costly than a misplay by an infielder. If the second baseman boots a ground ball, the batter usually gets one base. If an outfielder misplays a ground ball, the batter will get at least two bases, and maybe more. The other factor that must be considered is the level of competition. The higher the level, the more important the outfield play. The young man who wants to play the outfield in college or professional baseball must have defensive ability equal to that of any other player.

The requirements for the exceptional outfielder are just as demanding as they would be for players in other positions. He must be able to catch fly balls. To do this, he must learn to run on his toes rather than his heels. Running on the heels jars his spine and brings a blurring of the vision that can cause him to misjudge a fly ball. You, as the coach, must take careful note of how each player runs in the outfield. Teach him to get on the balls of his feet and to run that way all the time.

The outfielder is always running. If he is not chasing a fly ball or running to block a hard ground ball, he is running to help one of the other fielders by backing him up. An outfielder must always be in proper position if a thrown or batted ball gets by one of the infielders.

Shoes are important to the outfielder since he does so much running. He should take care of his shoes and always keep them in good shape for games. The spikes should fit him snugly, being at least one size smaller than his street shoes. The spike plates should not be loose or about to become loose, and the shoes should not be split open or about to fall apart. It is best to have two pairs of shoes, one for practice and one in which to play.

QUALIFICATIONS

An outfielder must have exceptional *self-discipline*. Since the ball does not come his way very often, he can get into a habit of not concentrating. Playing the outfield is not a stationary job. On the contrary, an efficient outfielder knows the meaning of the word "hustle." He must be alert to what is going on at all times and discipline himself always to keep his mind on the game.

He must have good *speed*. Although this qualification is particularly important for the centerfielder, it is also desirable in the left and rightfielder. There is a great deal of space from foul line to foul line, and a slow outfielder can create quite a gap in a team's defense.

An outfielder needs a *strong arm*. Needless to say, outfielders have to be able to throw farther than any other player, and a weak throwing arm would be a severe handicap. The center and rightfielder should have exceptional throwing arms because of the distance they must throw.

Intelligence is another essential for successful outfield play, since many quick decisions must be made concerning the distance the batted ball will travel, when to try a shoestring catch, and to what base the ball should be thrown. The outfielder should know his pitchers as well as the hitters. Each pitcher has a style of pitching which affects the way each outfielder will play the hitters.

The centerfielder should be the most skilled outfielder because he has the largest territory to cover. Exceptional running speed is the key to greatness in center field. The player with the strongest arm should be placed in right field to prevent the scoring play from second to home, or the extra base from second to third on a single to right field. The leftfielder needs reasonable speed, a strong arm, and the ability to judge curving line drives.

STANCE

Outfielders use two basic types of stance: the "square" and the "drop-step." In the "square" stance, used also by infielders, the outfielder faces the hitter, his feet parallel and comfortably separated, with his weight on the balls of his feet (Fig. 12-1). In the "drop-step," the outfielder also faces the batter, but he places the toe of the rear foot even with the heel of the front foot (Fig. 12-2). The expected direction of the ball determines which foot is dropped back. This position enables the player to get a quicker jump on the ball. The "drop-step," which allows an easy backward or forward movement, is the one most frequently used today. In either stance, the foot farthest from the ball generally takes the first step, a cross-over in the direction of the ball.

A frequent mistake of outfielders is keeping their hands on their knees when the pitcher delivers the ball. Although they may rest in this position, the hands should be lifted when the pitcher starts his windup, thus making them ready to move in any direction.

THROWING

Throwing is another important skill. Every batter and every runner creates a different situation. The outfielder must prevent batters from taking that extra base as well as nail runners who overrun or tag up.

The ideal outfield throw is low and fast. It should be made overhand and, unless the distance is short, should reach the base on one hop. The ball should be gripped across the seams to achieve the best carry and to eliminate curves.

All relay throws should reach the cutoff man chest high. If he gives the outfielder an accurate line, the ball should bounce or hop to the base or plate. Do not fail to impress upon the outfielder that he must hit the cutoff man with a low throw. If it is apparent that the runner will reach base easily, the cutoff man still can make a play on another advancing runner. A low throw may enable him to change the direction of the play. An outfielder should never lob the ball or hold on to it.

An outfielder should consider every possible play before each pitch is made. As each batter comes to the plate, he should survey the situation—men on base, outs, inning, score, the base runner's habits, and the probable direction of the ball. After

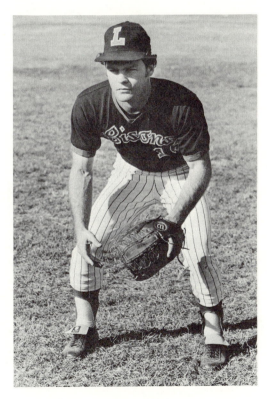

Figure 12-1

evaluting all the facts and possibilities and deciding upon the most logical procedure, he is ready. If he waits until the ball is on its way before determining the proper play, he will delay his throw and possibly throw to the wrong base.

An outfielder should remember that sometimes it is more advantageous to prevent a runner from getting into a scoring position than to keep another man from scoring. The percentage of putouts at the plate on outfield throws is small. The score, the inning, the number of outs and how the ball is hit will determine if a play should be made at the plate. When balls are hit to the left or right of the outfielder, he usually does not have a play at the plate, if the runner is attempting to score from second base. He should always be aware of the percentages involved in making an attempt to throw out a runner.

Figure 12-2

You may have noticed that many outfielders get a stronger throw when they are moving toward the diamond. Sometimes the outfielder will have to hop into throwing position to get full strength into the throw. But when he is handling a routine fly ball, it is a good idea to give himself a little extra room, moving back away from the spot where the catch will be made, and then catching the ball on the move. While moving, he can get off a quick, powerful throw without extra windup or hop. This is the mark of an experienced outfielder.

If the outfielder is throwing correctly, his throwing arm is away from his body so he can bring the ball back and throw it in one continuous motion. The elbow comes back first, and the forearm comes straight down, pointing to the ground. Then, as the elbow leads the way, the arm, wrist, and hand are brought

Figure 12-3

forward. The throwing arm is whipped through in a free movement, coming straight forward and then down across the body.
The entire body follows through to get the necessary power behind the throw (Fig. 12-3).

FIELDING

The aggressive outfielder is expecting each pitch to be hit in
his direction. In his mind he has gone over each possible play,
and he knows what to do with the ball when he receives it. The
general idea is to throw the ball ahead of the runner, when there
is no one else on base.

The outfielder's primary job is catching flies and grounders
cleanly. Line drives and flies hit directly over his head are his
two most difficult plays.

On liners, he should keep his eyes on the ball constantly. If
he is not sure about his first step, he should take one step backward. An inexperienced outfielder who takes a step forward
when he is uncertain often finds the ball carrying over his head.
Constant practice is needed to curb the instinct to charge forward on all liners. It is understood, of course, that the outfielder
will charge all balls that he is sure will remain in front of him.

In catching a fly hit over his head, an outfielder should turn
and run to the spot where he thinks the ball will descend. If
possible, he should get in front of the ball; if not, he should make
the catch over his shoulder. Always, he should run on the balls of
his feet, not on his heels.

If an outfielder is weak on this play, he should glue his eyes
on the ball from the time it leaves the bat; however, in practices,
he should turn his back on all such plays until he perfects the
technique. Having someone throw balls over the outfielder's
head is a helpful practice drill.

There are two methods of fielding grounders—the infielder
method and the knee on the ground. The proper choice depends
on the game situation and the ground conditions. If the winning
run is on second base in a late inning, the outfielder must charge
the grounder and try to make a play at the plate. This is a
desperation play, a do-or-die effort.

Unfortunately, very few outfielders spend enough time
fielding ground balls. Most coaches do not devote enough prac-

tice to charging grounders—drills in which players must field the ball and throw quickly and accurately. This play requires practice and must become a habit. My observation is that most errors in the outfield occur on ground balls.

If the tying run is scoring in this situation, the outfielder may throw to the plate, or, if the runner obviously cannot be headed off, to second base to keep the winning run from advancing to second. This choice will depend on your philosophy, the number of outs, which is the home team, and where the ball is hit. The outfielder must therefore be as alert as the catcher or the infielders.

On a ground ball hit to the outfield with the bases empty, the outfielder should play it safe by blocking the ball with one knee on the ground, the one on the same side as the player's throwing arm—right-handed thrower, right knee (Fig. 12-4).

Figure 12-4

Whether an outfielder can come in fast enough to catch a ball in front of him creates another tough problem. When his team has a comfortable lead, even if there are runners in scoring position, sometimes it is advisable to make an attempt. The shoestring catch is a gamble, though, and outfielders should learn the art of blocking the ball when they cannot make the catch. The left and rightfielder should remember that the pulled ball will hook toward the foul line and the sliced ball will veer away from the batter's normal line of power.

Every outfielder is aware of the difficulty that arises when a fly ball is hit in "neutral" territory. This situation is underscored when one drops safely because each of the outfielders thought the other had it. The average fan does not realize how many games are lost by such pop flies falling for base hits.

The aggressive outfielder goes after each fly ball in his territory as though he can make the play. He calls "loudly" for any that he can catch. He should never assume that the other fielders can make the play but should be aggressive in his own play. Waving one's arms is not a sufficient method of communication. Whenever there might be some question as to who should field a fly ball, both outfielders and infielders should be communicating with one another. When two or more players arrive within reach of the ball, the man who yells "I have it" takes the ball, and the others give him the right of way. The player should call loudly enough that everyone in the area can hear him, and he should continue to yell "I have it" until the catch is made. At Lipscomb we require the fielder to yell at least twice if he plans to make the catch. The outfielder has preference over the infielder if both men call for the ball, but if the infielder calls first, the outfielder should allow him to make the play.

The centerfielder should have preference on balls hit to right-center field or left-center field. You should place your best fielder in center because more balls are hit to that position than to either of the other two outfield positions. Thus, it would make sense to have the centerfielder field all the balls that he can get to. If two outfielders call for the ball, the centerfielder has the right-of-way, and the other outfielders should get out of his way. If the outfielders and infielders remember these cardinal points, they will minimize this difficulty.

Since most parks have a sun field, it is very important for each outfielder to have some experience playing with the sun in his face. The wise coach will buy a few pairs of special baseball sun glasses, which fit around the head with an elastic band. The player needs merely to tap the peak of his cap for them to flip into place (Fig. 12-5). These sun glasses will increase an outfielder's chances of catching balls coming out of the sun.

Figure 12-5

BACKING UP THE INFIELD

The art of backing up on all thrown or batted balls is one of the most difficult for the outfielder to master. It requires a great deal of hustle and aggressive outfield play.

The outfielder must be "heads up" whenever there are men on base and where there is a possibility of an infielder-to-infielder throw. Until he perfects this area of play, he can never hope to become an excellent outfielder.

The leftfielder backs up second on all plays from the right side. He backs up third base on all bunts, pickoffs, and rundowns. He should back up third base when a bunted ball is played to first base for a possible return throw to third. The centerfielder backs up second on all bunts and plays at that base. The rightfielder backs up first on all bunts, pickoff plays, and throws made there. He backs up second on all throws from the left side. On rundowns between first and second, he should move in quickly and back up first base.

On ground balls, the outfielders should assume that the infielder will miss the ball and go to a back-up position. They must be thinking of every possible play that could be made by the defense and how they can contribute to the overall team play.

Playing the outfield is not an easy job. Those individuals who have the desire to be outfielders must realize that excellence comes only from many hours of hard work.

GETTING THE JUMP

The outfielder with the fastest start will catch the most balls. In order to get the "good jump," the outfielder must be ready to move in any direction as the ball leaves the bat. Getting a jump on the ball is mostly a matter of practice—constant practice which will develop experience. When the outfielder gains this experience, he will have a sense of where the ball is going.

You must teach the outfielder to concentrate on the hitter, since this is the key to getting the jump on the ball. He must be ready to make his move the instant the ball is hit. Even though he is a great distance from the plate, the experienced outfielder can tell where the ball is going when it is hit. He must be ready on every pitch.

On any ball at which the hitter has swung the bat— whether he missed or hit foul—the outfielder should be moving. If he does not move in this situation, he is not in the game. The outfielder learns to move and get the jump during batting practice. He should be bearing down during this period and profiting most from practice.

The outfielder must know the wind direction. The best way to test wind direction is to throw some grass into the air and see which way it carries. The wind often changes during the course of a game; so the outfielder should check it each inning.

In order to get the fastest start possible in the outfield, the crossover step is used. If the ball is hit to the right, the outfielder pursues it by crossing the left foot over the right (Fig. 12-6). The opposite applies on balls hit to the outfielder's left.

The toughest ball to get a jump on is the line drive directly at the outfielder. It is difficult to tell if it will sink or rise, because he has no side view. This make it difficult to tell how hard the ball is hit.

Figure 12-6

You should teach your outfielders to catch the ball with two hands. Since so many players are using the large glove with long fingers and considerable webbing, they like to catch the ball one-handed. This is not a recommended practice, since the one-handed catch makes it more difficult to get off a good throw. It takes time to reach up into the glove, take the ball out, and throw it. If the ball is caught with two hands, not only is there less chance of dropping it, but the player is in position to throw it immediately.

The outfielder should develop the habit of catching the ball the same way every time. The best place to catch a fly ball is off the shoulder of the throwing arm. This is the quickest way to get the ball out of the glove and throw it all in one motion.

PLAYING THE FENCE

All outfielders should know how the ball will rebound from fences or walls. Many high school and college baseball fields have fences; yet this phase of outfield play is rarely mentioned by the coach. Every fence is different, and before the game the outfielder should check how the ball will carom off of it.

On fly balls near the fence, the outfielder should turn and run as fast as he can toward it. Then he is ready to play the ball without worrying about the fence. Even if he has to come back toward the infield several feet, he is in a better position to throw. This procedure is much better than backing up into the fence. When the outfielder is backing up, he is not sure when he will hit it, and he usually plays too cautiously. The secret to the play is really hustling to the fence when the ball is first hit.

The outfielder should always move quickly on all fly balls. He should never "drift" with a fly ball. Too many young outfielders fall into this habit. It is not good technique.

During batting practice, have a fungo batter hit several balls against the wall for the outfielder to learn how to determine the manner in which the ball will rebound.

Generally speaking, the outfielder is called upon to make only a limited number of defensive plays during a game. To make the most of each opportunity, he must use intelligence and hustle. Consequently, intelligence and hustle are the major traits to look for when choosing an outfielder.

POINTS TO REMEMBER

1. Always play a ground ball safely, blocking it if necessary, when the bases are empty.

2. Watch the opponents in batting practice and make an analysis of each hitter.

3. Check the wind and sun at the start of each inning.

4. Always run on the toes when catching a fly ball.

5. Know when a pitchout or pickoff is called, and make a fast start to back up the play.

6. Never give up on a fly ball.

7. Try to face the ball when making the catch.

8. Know the speed of every runner.

9. Always throw ahead of the runner to prevent an advance.

10. Try to catch every fly on the throwing arm side.

11. Remember, if a batted ball to right or left is curving, it always curves toward the foul line.

12. Know the score, the inning, the number of outs, and the strengths and weaknesses of the opponent.

13. Charge all grounders, even if intending merely to block them.

14. Move away from the pull position with two strikes on the hitter.

15. Never hold the ball with runners on base.

16. Make one-bounce throws to all bases except in close range.

17. Back up all throws from one infielder to another.

18. Move with every pitch.

19. Take all flies which can be handled either by an infielder or an outfielder, except when the infielder calls first.

20. Work out in the infield to learn to handle grounders.

13

SECRETS OF CHAMPIONSHIP DEFENSIVE PLAY

The successful execution of championship defensive strategy depends upon the coordinated effort of several players. Defensive strategy is a matter of team defense rather than individual defense. A team is rarely stronger than its defense. Perfection of individual skills and coordination of these skills into team play are the real essentials of defense as a whole. Each defensive player must have and use a comprehensive knowledge of various baseball situations and of other conditions on the field which affect his defensive play. He must keep the following facts in mind: the score, the inning, the count on the batter, the number of outs, and the capabilities of the offensive players.

Every defensive player should plan what he will do if the next pitch is hit to him. If each player thoughtfully reviews all the possible plays that can occur in a given play situation, he will not make mental mistakes. Defense is based upon two factors: 1. each player in the right place at the right time; 2. each player aware of what he must do with the ball when it is hit to him.

TEAM DEFENSE

The defensive positions of infielders and outfielders usually depend on the stage of the game and the ability of the batter. If the situation in the game warrants playing back with a straight-away hitter at bat, the defense plays deep and is concentrated toward the middle of the diamond. In defending against a right-handed pull batter or a left-handed opposite-field batter, the defense swings toward the left-field line, and the left-field side of the defense plays deeper than the right. The defense is swung similarly toward the right-field line for a left-handed pull hitter or a right-handed opposite-field hitter.

When the stage of the game warrants playing in for the purpose of making a play at the plate, the defense moves forward to a position where the infielders are on the baseline or on the edge of the infield grass. It is here that one of the most frequent and most serious violations of sound defensive positioning is made. The practice of playing the infield in close to cut off a run at the plate whenever the opposition has a man on third is defi-nitely overused, sometimes to the point of folly. An attempt should be made to cut down the man at the plate only if a really important run is involved—never in the early innings when there is plenty of opportunity to get back the run. If the defense plays in, the opponent's .200 hitter becomes a .400 hitter, and the gates are opened for a big inning.

The "medium" position of the infield should be used during the middle innings when it is desirable to prevent a run, but not to the extent of leaving the infield vulnerable to ground balls that may go through and set up the big inning. In late innings the "medium" position is employed when the batter lacks speed, the runner on third is fast, a double-play situation exists, and the infield is capable of making the double play. It must be kept in mind here that the infielders may play "deep," "medium," or "short" as individuals rather than as a unit. A widely used in-field setup is to have the shortstop and the second baseman at "medium" depth and the first and the third baseman "deep." It is frequent strategy also to play the first and the third baseman "in close" to make the play at the plate, while the shortstop and the second baseman stay in the medium position, going for the double play.

When a team is being met for the first time and no advance information is available concerning the various players, each player is considered a straight-away hitter. Definite conclusions often are reached in this matter by watching the pre-game practice. In fact, batting practice should be watched, even though the team has been played previously or has been scouted, because there is always the possibility that some batter may reveal a flagrant weakness that has been overlooked. Also, a recheck can then be made as to where the various players hit the ball. The watching should involve all players and coaches.

The forward and backward movement of the defense should be controlled by you because if players are allowed to shift themselves some may play in and others back under the same conditions. If possible, decisions should be made prior to the start of the game, so that the infielders and outfielders will know where to play as soon as the batter steps to the plate. You can often alter the position of various players during the course of the game, but because of your many duties, it is impossible for you to do so throughout the game. For this reason it is important for the defensive players to know where each batter is likely to hit the ball and to move accordingly. This should be done as a unit to give the defense balance.

DEFENSIVE POSITIONS

FIRST BASEMAN

Depending upon his ability to go right or left, the first baseman's normal position is eight to fifteen feet from the foul line, and fifteen to twenty-five feet back of the line between first and second base. The hitter's tendency to pull the ball must be taken into consideration. The first baseman plays on the base with first or first and third bases occupied, except when a runner is not likely to attempt a steal. In this case, the first baseman stands a few steps behind the runner.

INFIELDERS

The second baseman's normal position is twenty to thirty feet back of the line between first and second base; the short-stop's is the same distance back of the line between second and third base. The third baseman's position is ten to twenty feet back of the line between second and third base.

The third baseman plays in the short position when a sacrifice bunt is expected with fewer than two outs and until two strikes are called against the batter who might bunt. He should play in this position also when a weak-hitting player has two strikes charged against him, and the situation warrants a bunt. The first and the second basemen may move a few steps toward the batter for the same reason. If a bunt is attempted to move a runner to third base, the first baseman plays a few steps in front of the short position, and the shortstop stays close to second base to shorten the lead of the runner.

When there is a possibility of a steal of second base, the shortstop and the second baseman must agree on who will cover the base. The player covering should move in two or three steps toward the batter and a few steps toward second base. This position permits delaying the start to cover until the ball is hit or passes the batter. It also places the player in position to cover quickly on a delayed steal. In most situations with a runner on first base, the shortstop and second baseman will be in double-play position.

If an intentional pass is being issued, the player who normally covers second base takes a deep position, and the other player who forms the keystone combination plays on the base. This protects against a careless pitch, in which case the ball is more likely to be hit to the opposite field.

DOUBLE PLAY DEFENSE

In a double play situation, the same pattern of shifts for each type of hitter should be followed, but the infield plays closer to the batter.

The shortstop and the second baseman move a few steps nearer the plate and second base to increase the chances for a double play. The only exception is a batter who definitely is known as a pull hitter. In this situation, the fielder on the side to which the batter hits plays the batter, placing himself somewhat deeper than for a normal double play.

The first baseman's position varies from approximately ten feet behind the first-to-second baseline to five feet ahead of that line. If he is holding a runner on first base, he should break toward second base as the pitch is delivered.

The third baseman plays from approximately ten feet behind the second-to-third baseline all the way to the line, depending upon the type of hitter. A strong pull hitter requires a deeper defensive position than a straightaway hitter.

OTHER FACTORS

Each player takes a defensive position according to his own fielding ability. If an infielder cannot go to the right as well as to the left or vice versa, he should play a few steps to the weak side. For a similar reason, a slow outfielder plays deeper than one that has speed. The inability to go back for balls is another weakness against which some outfielders must protect themselves.

The power and speed of the batter are also taken into consideration. When known hard hitters are batting, the defense plays deep, and if known weak hitters are at the plate, the infield moves in closer. This is doubly true for outfielders because of the large areas they must cover. The infielders must consider the speed with which the batter reaches first base. Fast, quick-breaking players are not played as deeply as those who are slow in reaching the base. Most left-handed batters come under the fast group, since they bat from a position closer to first base.

In some cases the defensive positions are influenced by the pitcher's control and speed. A pitcher who depends on the fast ball for success usually causes the batter to hit late. On the other hand, the pitcher who relies on curves and control will find the batter pulling the ball most of the time.

The defensive position of the infielders may be affected by

the condition of the field. Some infields are harder and faster than others and require a deeper defensive position. Some grass infields slow the ball down to such a degree that the infielders should play in a medium position. In the pre-game warmup, each defensive player should check the area he must cover. It is important to smooth rough places on the ground and remove obstacles such as rocks and paper. These may affect the fielding of ground balls.

THE RUNDOWN

Every baseball team must have a planned defense against offensive players caught in a rundown. Many plans have merit, but the double and the single rotation will be discussed in this chapter.

In the double rotation system, the fundamental rule for each player is always to follow his throw, except when the pitcher picks a runner off second base.

If the pitcher picks a runner off first base, he hustles to first and gets behind the base, since he will not be in the play, if executed properly. If it is not executed correctly, he will move up to the base, receive the ball, and tag the runner. The pitcher should stay out of the play if possible, because this minimizes the chance of injury.

As soon as the first baseman catches the ball, he should run toward the base runner. As soon as the shortstop is in position, the first baseman throws the ball to him and follows the throw to second base. The fundamental rule here is always to rotate to the right. The second baseman should go toward first base as soon as he sees the runner is picked off. He should cut in sharply behind the runner about ten feet from first base, in position to receive the throw from the shortstop. As soon as the shortstop receives the throw from the first baseman, he runs the runner toward first base as hard as he can. As the runner gets within a few feet of the second baseman, the throw is made by the shortstop. The second baseman may have to take a few steps forward quickly to tag the runner. Since the runner is going full speed toward first base, it will be impossible for him to stop and start in a new direction before being tagged out. When the shortstop throws to the second baseman or pitcher, he should continue on to first base, in case the runner is not retired. Two throws should be the maximum number required to put a runner out.

If a runner has been picked off second base, the shortstop or the second baseman, whoever takes the throw, runs him hard toward third base. The pitcher immediately goes to third base, and the third baseman moves up the baseline several feet. As the runner approaches the third baseman, the player making the play throws the ball, rotates to his right, and follows the throw. The third baseman should have time to tag the runner before he can change directions. If this play is executed properly, the runner should be put out in one throw. Some coaches do not like running the base runner hard away from the base from which he was picked off. If this is true, get the ball to the third baseman and let him run the base runner hard toward second base. The throw then will go to the shortstop or the second baseman, whoever is left, and the runner should be tagged out in two throws.

If a runner is caught off third base by the ball being hit to the pitcher, the pitcher should run directly toward him. This will make him commit himself, preferably toward third, and it is an easy matter to throw him out. The first baseman backs up the catcher at home plate, and the shortstop backs up the play at third base. As soon as the pitcher throws either to third or home, he backs up that base.

If the pitcher picks the runner off third, he should back up that base. The first baseman goes to home plate and the shortstop to third. The third baseman chases the runner several yards toward the plate and throws to the catcher, who runs full speed at him and throws to the shortstop for the putout. The shortstop should be several feet in front of third base and in a position to make the tag before the runner has time to change directions.

In the single rotation system, only one player rotates, while the other players remain stationary. When the pitcher picks the runner off first base, he immediately backs up that base. The first baseman throws the ball to the second baseman and remains stationary. The shortstop backs up the second baseman.

The second baseman runs hard toward the runner and throws the ball when the runner is in position to be tagged out by the first baseman. If necessary, the second baseman rotates to the right. This play has the shortstop and the second baseman on one end and the first baseman on the other, while the pitcher backs up first.

If the runner is picked off second base, the shortstop and the second baseman handle second and rotate, while the third baseman remains stationary. The pitcher backs up third base.

If the runner is picked off third base, the shortstop goes to third. The third baseman rotates, and the catcher remains stationary. The pitcher goes where the throw is made, and the first baseman covers home with the catcher.

The important things to remember in all run-downs are: get the runner going full speed, throw the ball no more than two times, hold the ball up in a throwing position, and do not let the runner make contact with a defensive infielder. It should be pointed out that if a runner breaks fast to the next base the ball should be thrown immediately to that base. There is a growing trend among coaches toward eliminating any fakes on the part of the infielders involved. If a fake is used, it is recommended that only one full arm fake be made.

PICKOFF PLAYS

Pickoff plays deserve considerable discussion, since they can be exactly effective in games in which the score is close. Falling victim to a well-executed pickoff play not only places the runner in an embarrassing position but also erases his scoring potential. A team that makes use of a reservoir of applicable pickoff plays can accomplish the following: 1. erase potential runs; 2. force opposing runners to be honest; 3. lessen the defensive pressure; 4. enjoy a psychological advantage; 5. create greater defensive alertness.

The plays that will be explained have been identified by names which best describe the action required and the base involved in the play. The coach may have a vocal signal with which to start the play or alert the player who has the responsibility of initiating it.

FIRST-BASE PICKOFF

Runners are on first and second base with fewer than two outs and preferably a tight-handed hitter at the plate. The first baseman or the catcher initiates the play with a prearranged signal.

The first baseman plays very deep. As the pitcher starts his delivery, the first baseman breaks directly at the runner and then turns sharply to the base. The catcher, who generally calls for a breaking pitch or a pitchout away from the right-handed hitter, then makes the throw to first.

It is amazing how many first base coaches will watch the pitch to the plate; and therein lies the key to the success of the play.

CATCHER'S CHOICE AT FIRST

With a runner on first base and a sacrifice bunt situation anticipated, this play may work. It is called by the catcher. Upon receiving the signal, the pitcher will pitch wide, so the batter is unable to bunt the ball. As the pitcher goes into his stretch, the first baseman rushes in for the expected bunt. The second baseman leaves his position to take the throw at first. He should run to a point a few feet back of first base, so he may approach the bag parallel to the baseline. In this position he is better able to shift his feet should the throw be wide, and he can make the tag more easily.

BACK-UP PLAY AT FIRST

If a bunt is expected with a runner on first only and the pickoff signal is given, the first baseman takes several running steps toward the plate as the pitch is made, luring the runner a step or two from the base. Just before the ball reaches the batter, the first baseman whirls back to the base to receive the throw from the catcher. The same play can be used when a bunt is not expected, except the first baseman takes several running steps toward second base as the pitch is made and then hustles back to first just before the ball reaches the batter.

PITCHER TO FIRST BASE

The runner on first base shows poor leadoff techniques by crossing the legs or dashing off the base at the wrong time. The first baseman gets the attention of the pitcher and calls the play. As the pitcher takes his stretch, he throws to first base while his arms are in the process of moving downward. Since most base runners take their lead while the pitcher is stretching, the throw to first will catch the runner leaning toward second base.

THE JOCKEY PICKOFF

When there is a runner on second base, the shortstop initiates the play by breaking two or three steps toward second base. The pitcher glances at the shortstop, who stops and then continues on to the base. The pitcher should whirl as the shortstop starts the second time. The throw should be timed so the ball and the shortstop reach the base at the same time. If the shortstop starts and then returns to his position, the pitcher glances at the second baseman, who has taken a few steps toward second and breaks for the base, when the runner begins to move toward third. If the second baseman does not break for the base, the pitcher delivers to the batter. The coach must make sure it is understood that there will be only one break to the base by each infielder. If the pitcher knows this, he will not pitch with either infielder out of position.

THE COUNT METHOD

The shortstop gives the signal for this play, and the pitcher answers. The pitcher moves into the set position, and, as his arms come to rest in front of his body, he starts counting—one, two, three. On the count of three, he whirls and throws to second base. The shortstop also starts counting when the pitcher comes to the set position and breaks for the base on two. Timing is very important on this play.

PICK AT SECOND

This play is used when a runner on second is taking a long, careless lead. The shortstop gives the signal to the pitcher and the second baseman. When the pitcher steps on the rubber, he turns his head toward the shortstop, who has gone wide and close to the hole so the runner can see him and thus get off. In the meantime the second baseman has edged closer to second base. When the pitcher's foot contacts the rubber to take the stretch, the count begins. On the count of one, the second baseman breaks, and on three the pitcher turns to throw for the pickoff.

PICK AT THIRD

The play is used when a runner at third base is taking a long lead and you have a right-handed pitcher on the mound. The third baseman initiates the play by giving the signal to the pitcher. The pitcher must throw from the stretch. When he raises his left leg to make the throw to the plate, the third baseman breaks for the base, and the pitcher steps toward the base to make the throw to the third baseman. Since this is a very dangerous play, the third baseman must be sure the base runner is off far enough to be picked off. Timing is important, and this play will need several hours of practice.

It should be understood that a throw for a pickoff may be made any time the batter misses the ball in an attempt to bunt or hit, if in the catcher's judgment a throw has merit. The runner usually takes an extra step as he sees the batter attempt to make contact with the ball. Therefore, the infielders must hurry to their bases as soon as the ball passes the batter, ready for a throw from the catcher. A throw by the catcher or the pitcher should be knee high when the infielder receives it.

BASIC CUTOFF
AND RELAY PATTERNS

Basic cutoff plays are the backbone of good team defense. The importance of the cutoff man cannot be stressed too much. He must think quickly and diagnose plays instantly. When the opponents start running the bases, it is imperative for the defense to know exactly where to go and what to do. The defense cannot afford to make a mistake. Often a game is lost by a run that scored because a man advanced a base as a result of a poorly executed cutoff or relay play. Many of these mistakes result from erratic throwing on the part of the outfielders. They must understand that all throws toward the cutoff or the relay man should be low enough for him to handle. If a ball is hit between the outfielders, they can help each other by giving instructions, but they should never become the relay man.

Infielders should station themselves inside a base while watching the runner tag a base in making the turn. Their being inside the base has a tendency to make the runner take a wider turn, thus increasing the distance he travels toward the next base. The infielder must not interfere with the runner by being too close to the base.

On routine base hits and fly balls to the outfield with no one on base, the outfielders should form the habit of making *low, hard, one-hop* throws to second base. The shortstop should cover on balls hit to left and center, while the second baseman covers on balls hit to right.

Some teams use the pitcher exclusively as their cutoff man. This is not a sound procedure because the pitcher is not an infielder. He does not take infield practice and consequently cannot field the ball as well as one who does. There is also the danger that he may injure his arm by throwing from an unnatural position.

Some high school teams, for simplicity, employ the first baseman exclusively as their cutoff man. This procedure is all right except when he is playing deep. From this position he cannot possibly get to the cutoff position on a sharp single to left field. Because of this problem, the system discussed here uses both the third and the first baseman as cutoff men. The third baseman is the cutoff man on a single to left field, on a fly ball to left with a man on third, or men on second and third. In all other situations, if there is a possible play at home, the first baseman acts as the cutoff man.

The objective of the defense in all the situations which will be diagrammed and explained is to have every base covered, every base backed up, and a player in the relay or cutoff positions whenever necessary. There are some situations on the double cutoff when extra-base hits will require leaving first base open. It is preferable to leave first open rather than any other base.

When an infielder acts as the cutoff man on throws from the outfield, he takes a position about 50 feet in front of the base to which the play is likely to be made, and in line with the throw. He should hold his arms in the air to give the outfielder a good target, and listen for the player covering the base to call "cut." No call means "let the ball go." If the throw is definitely too late to catch the runner, the cutoff man advances toward the ball so that he can intercept it sooner.

The shortstop and the second baseman act as relay men on very long fly balls that elude the outfielders. The shortstop performs this duty on balls to the left-field side and the second baseman on those to the right-field side. This is done at a point between 100 and 150 feet from the outfielder catching or retrieving the ball. The arms are above the head, and the infielder should be in line with the base to which the throw is to be made. In relaying the throw, the pivot should be executed toward the glove hand after the ball is caught.

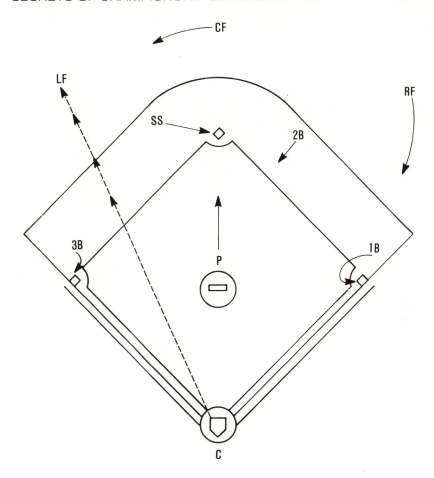

Diagram 13-1
Line Drive Single to Left Field, No One on Base

Situation

1. Pitcher moves toward second base in case ball is deflected.
2. Shortstop covers second base.
3. Second baseman backs up the base.
4. Right fielder backs up the throw to second.
5. Center fielder moves toward left field.

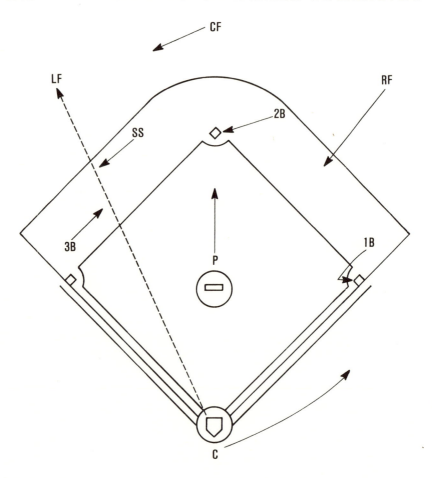

Diagram 13-2
Ground Ball Single to Left Field, No One on Base

Situation

1. Pitcher moves toward second base in case ball is deflected.
2. Shortstop goes after ground ball if there is a play.
3. Second baseman covers the base.
4. Right fielder backs up throw to second base.
5. Catcher follows runner down first baseline.

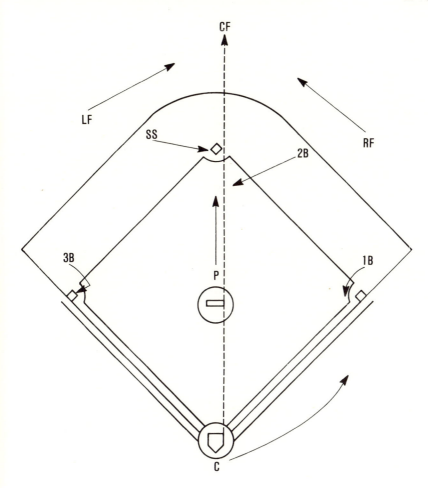

Diagram 13-3
Single to Center Field, No One on Base

Situation

1. Pitcher backs up throw to second base.
2. Catcher follows runner down line.
3. Shortstop covers second base.
4. Second baseman backs up the base.
5. Left and right fielders move toward center field.

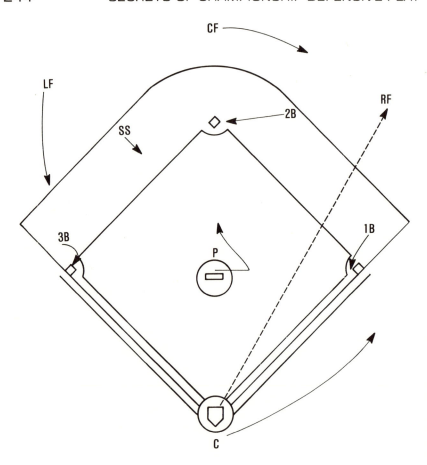

Diagram 13-4
Line Drive Single to Right Field, No One on Base

Situation

1. Pitcher moves toward first base until ball is past infielders, then moves toward second base.
2. Catcher follows runner down line.
3. Shortstop backs up the base.
4. Left fielder backs up the throw to second.

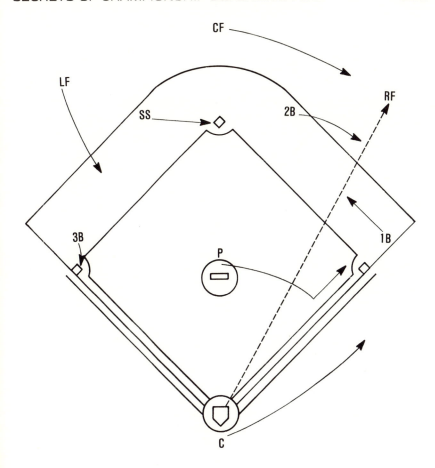

Diagram 13-5
Ground Ball Single to Right Field, No One on Base

Situation

1. Pitcher covers first base.
2. Catcher follows runner down line.
3. Shortstop covers second base.
4. Second baseman goes after ball.
5. Left fielder backs up the throw to second.

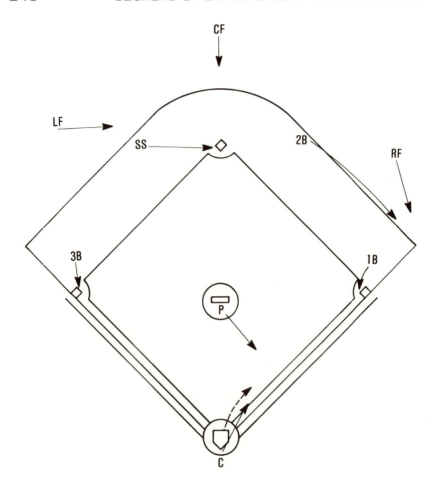

Diagram 13-6
Topped or Bunted Ball Near Home Plate,
No One on Base

Situation

1. Catcher fields ball and throws to first.
2. Pitcher moves toward the ball.
3. First baseman covers base.
4. Second baseman backs up first base.
5. Right fielder moves toward first base in case of overthrow.
6. Shortstop covers second base.

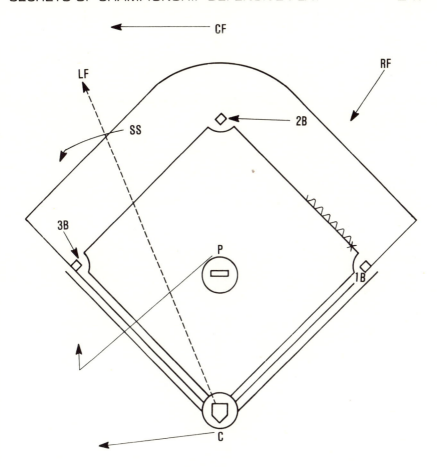

Diagram 13-7
Single to Left Field, Runner on First Base

Situation

1. Pitcher backs up third base.
2. Catcher moves in behind the pitcher, to back up the play.
3. Shortstop takes cutoff position in line with left fielder and third base.
4. Second baseman covers second.
5. Third baseman covers third.
6. Right fielder backs up possible throw to second base.

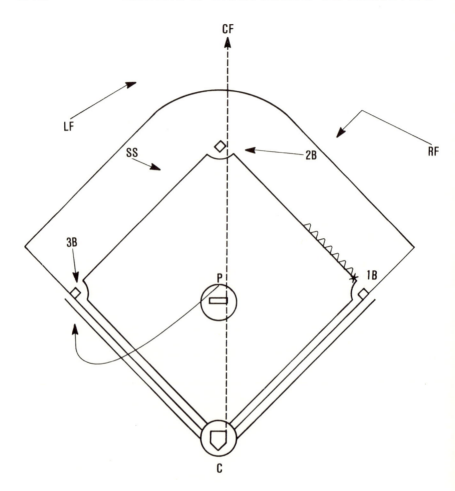

Diagram 13-8
Single to Center Field, Runner on First Base

Situation

1. Pitcher backs up third base.
2. Shortstop takes cutoff position in line with center fielder and third base.
3. Second baseman covers second.
4. Third baseman covers third.
5. Right fielder moves toward center field until ball is fielded cleanly, then moves to back up possible throw to second base.

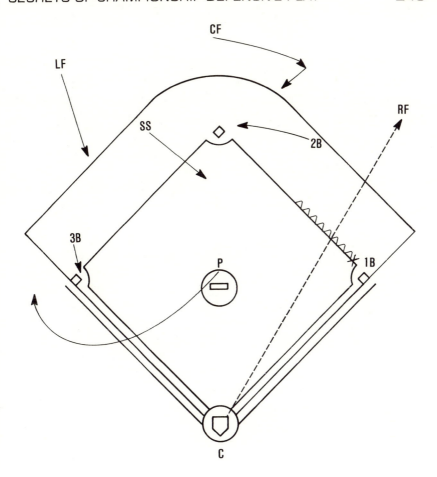

Diagram 13-9
Single to Right Field, Runner on First Base

Situation

1. Pitcher backs up third base.
2. Shortstop takes cutoff position in line with right field and third base.
3. Second baseman covers second.
4. Left fielder backs up possible throw to second base.
5. Center fielder moves toward right field until ball is fielded cleanly, then backs up possible throw to second base.

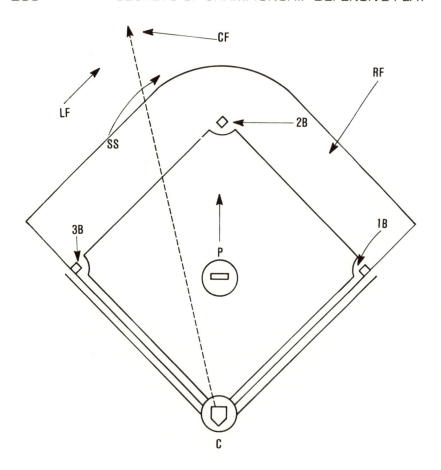

Diagram 13-10
Long Single, Possible Double, No One on Base

Situation

1. Pitcher moves toward second base.
2. Shortstop moves to relay position in outfield.
3. Second baseman covers the base at second.
4. Right fielder moves to a backup position behind second base.
5. Third baseman covers third.

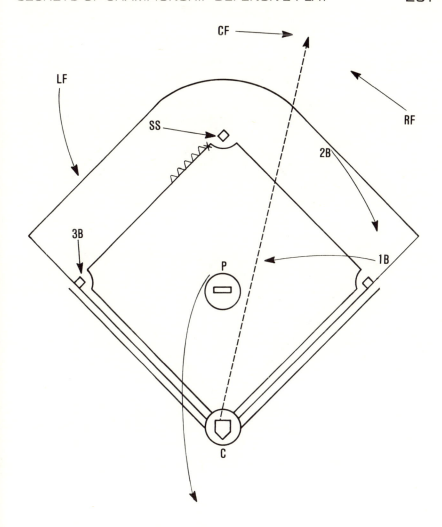

Diagram 13-11
Single to Right or Center, Second Base Occupied

Situation

1. Pitcher backs up home plate.
2. Shortstop covers second.
3. Second baseman covers first.
4. First baseman lines up throw to the plate.
5. Left fielder backs up possible throw to second base.

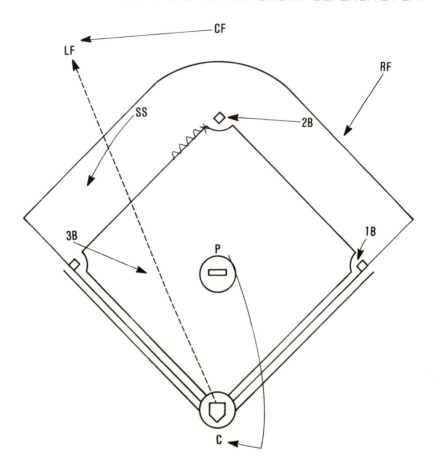

Diagram 13-12
Single to Left Field, Second Base Occupied

Situation

1. Pitcher backs up home plate.
2. Shortstop covers third base.
3. Second baseman covers second.
4. Third baseman lines up throw to plate.
5. Right fielder backs up possible throw to second base.

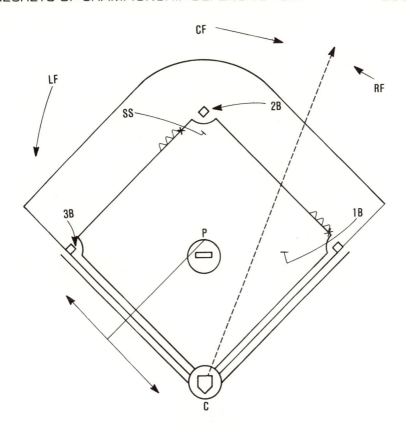

Diagram 13-13
Single to Right or Center Field with
First and Second Occupied

Situation

1. Pitcher breaks to point halfway between home and third base, sizing up the play and covering accordingly.
2. Shortstop lines up a possible throw to third from right or center field.
3. Second baseman covers second.
4. Third baseman covers third.
5. First baseman lines up possible throw to the plate. Score, inning, speed of ball hit, where ball is hit, strength of out-fielders' arm, and speed of base runners will determine where the ball will be thrown.

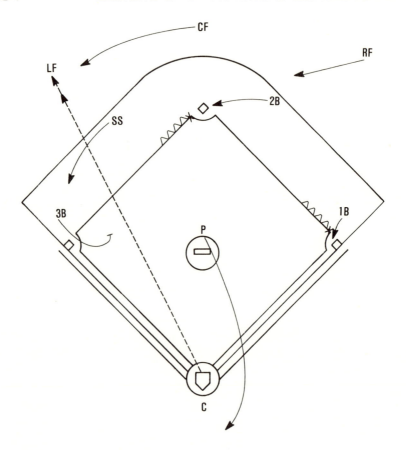

Diagram 13-14
Single to Left Field with First and Second Occupied

Situation

1. Pitcher backs up the plate.
2. Shortstop covers third base.
3. Second baseman covers second.
4. Third baseman lines up throw to plate.
5. Right fielder backs up possible throw to second base.

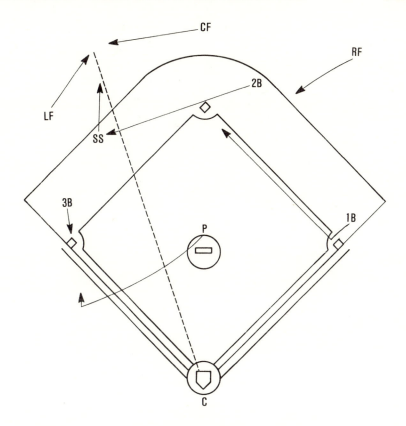

Diagram 13-15
Double, Possible Triple, to Left Center with No One on Base
(with man on second, man on third, or men on second and
third)

Situation

1. Pitcher backs up third base.
2. Shortstop moves to position in the outfield to be relay man. Follows the second baseman's instructions.
3. Second baseman moves to a position about 30 feet behind shortstop.
4. First baseman trails the runner to second base after moving toward base to make sure runner touches it.
5. Right fielder moves to position to back up second base.

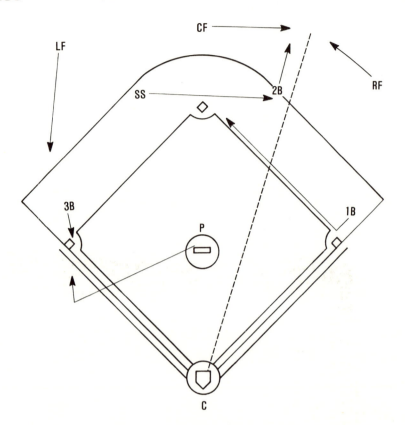

Diagram 13-16
Double, Possible Triple to Right Center with No One on Base
(with man on second, man on third, or men on second and
third)

Situation

1. Pitcher backs up third base.
2. Second baseman moves to a position in the outfield to be relay man. Follows the shortstop's instructions.
3. Shortstop moves to a position 30 feet behind the second baseman.
4. First baseman trails the runner to second base, after making sure runner touches base.
5. Left fielder moves toward third base to back up possible play.

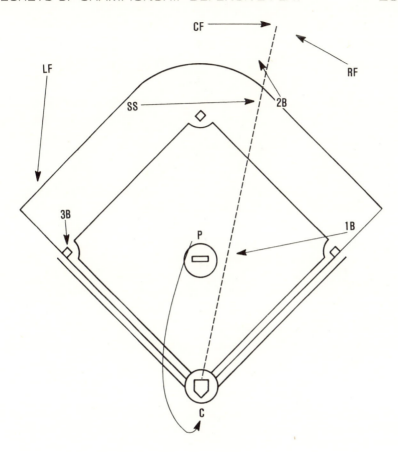

Diagram 13-17
Triple, Possible Inside-the-Park Home Run

Situation

1. Pitcher backs up home plate.
2. Second baseman moves to position in outfield to be relay man.
3. Shortstop backs up the second baseman, about thirty feet behind him.
4. First baseman moves to infield grass to the cutoff position.
5. Left fielder backs up third base for possible play.

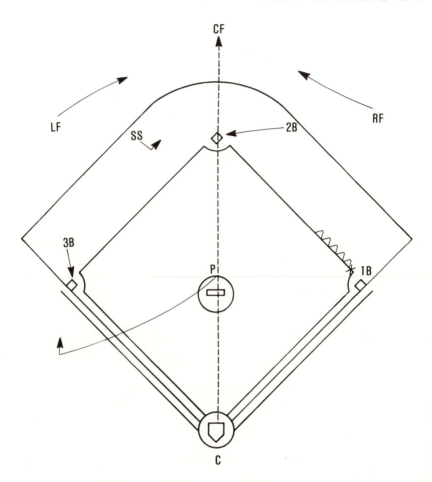

Diagram 13-18
Single to Center with a Man on First

Situation

1. Pitcher backs up third base.

2. Second baseman covers second.

3. Shortstop moves to position directly in line with the center fielder and third base.

4. Center fielder fields the ball and uses the shortstop as a guide for his throw to third.

5. Third baseman covers third base.

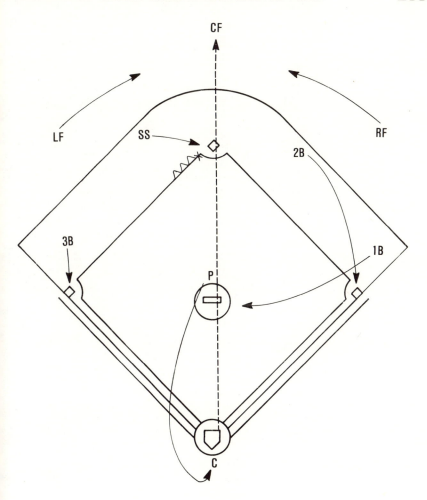

Diagram 13-19
Single to Center with Man on Second Base

Situation

1. Pitcher backs up home plate.
2. Second baseman covers first.
3. Shortstop covers second base.
4. First baseman moves to cutoff position in line with center field and home plate.
5. Third baseman covers third base.

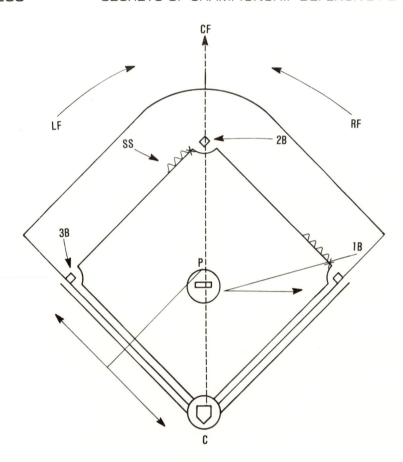

Diagram 13-20
Single to Center with Men on First and Second Base

Situation

1. Pitcher moves to a position halfway between third and home and backs up the base to which the throw is made.
2. First baseman moves to cutoff position for possible throw to the plate; if throw goes to third, he should move back to first.
3. Shortstop moves to position directly in line with center field and third base.
4. Second baseman covers second base.
5. Third baseman covers third base.

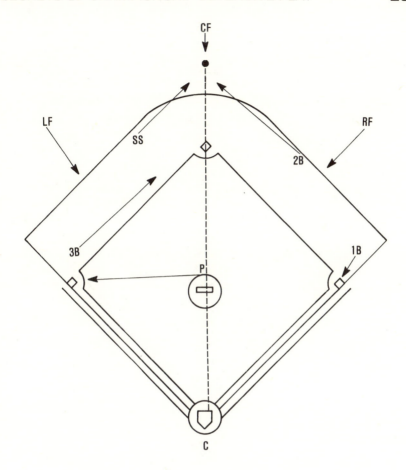

Diagram 13-21
Pop Fly Behind Second Base with No One on Base

Situation

1. Pitcher covers third base.
2. Shortstop and second baseman go after pop fly.
3. Center fielder goes after pop fly.
4. Third baseman covers second base.
5. First baseman covers first base.

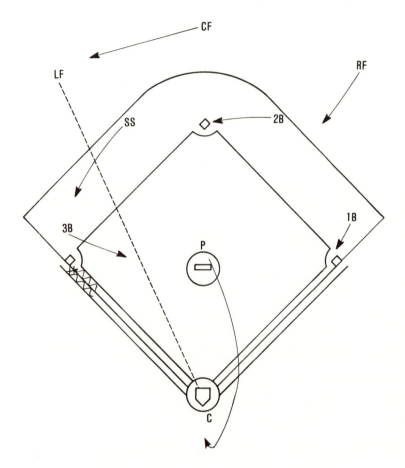

Diagram 13-22
Possible Sacrifice Fly to Left with Man on Third

Situation

1. Pitcher backs up home plate.
2. Shortstop covers third base.
3. Second baseman covers second.
4. Third baseman moves to cutoff position in line with left field and home plate.
5. Right fielder backs up second base in case left fielder drops the ball and throws to second.

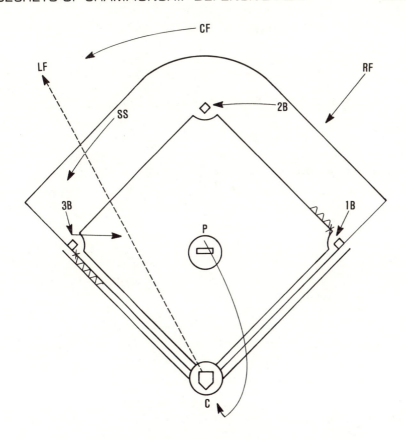

Diagram 13-23
Possible Sacrifice Fly to Left with Men on
First and Third

Situation

1. Pitcher backs up home plate.
2. Shortstop covers third base.
3. Second baseman covers second.
4. Third baseman moves toward third base, then in line with left fielder and home plate for possible cutoff.
5. Left fielder catches the ball and makes decision concerning throw to plate or second base.
6. Right fielder backs up second base.

   An accurate throw and a properly positioned cutoff man will keep the runner on first from moving to second.

CHAMPIONSHIP BUNT DEFENSE

Two bunt situations for which a team must perfect a defense are a runner on first base and runners on first and second base, with the bunt in order. There are other situations, but these two must be defensed, or the team will be in constant trouble.

When a runner is on first base with no one out, the third baseman should be alert for a possible bunt. The shortstop and second baseman should play the double-play position, while the first baseman holds the runner on base. If the ball is bunted, the pitcher fields it if it is in front of him or to his left. The third baseman will field it if it is bunted to the pitcher's right and down the third baseline. The catcher should field any bunt near home plate. If the pitcher or the third baseman fields the ball, the catcher should call the base to which the throw should be made. If the third baseman fields the ball, the catcher or the pitcher should cover third base. Some teams let the third baseman sprint back to third after fielding the ball, to prevent the runner from first base going to third. But this is a difficult play for the third baseman, since he is moving away from the base when he fields the ball. If the pitcher or the catcher fields the bunt, the third baseman has adequate time to cover his base. The outfielders should back up the bases in case of a bad throw.

When runners are on first and second base with one or no outs and the situation calls for a bunt, the first and the third basemen play in. The shortstop and the second baseman can play at the double play position, but the second baseman must be sure he can cover first base. The pitcher must field the ball if bunted to his right, since the third baseman covers third base. The first baseman charges in and fields the ball if bunted on the first-base side of the mound. The second baseman covers first base, and the shortstop covers second. If the ball is bunted sharply down the third-base side, the third baseman should field it and make the play to first. He should not charge forward until he sees the ball will get by the pitcher (Diag. 13-24). The pitcher and the third baseman must work together on this play. The pitcher should let the third baseman know when he is able to field the bunt. If he does not do this, the third baseman may charge the ball too quickly, and no one will be covering third if the pitcher fields the bunted ball.

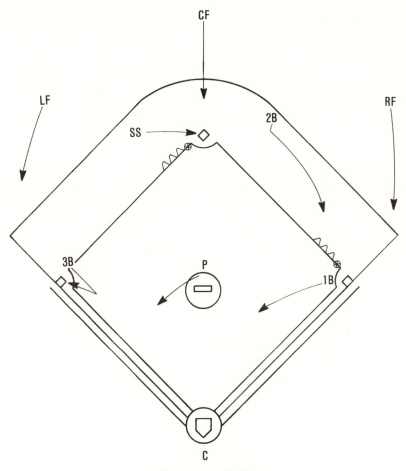

Diagram 13-24

When the pitcher takes his stretch, he should watch the shortstop and deliver the ball when he fakes the runner back into second base. This prevents the runner from getting a big lead and makes possible the force play at third base. If the runner takes a long lead, the pitcher should throw to the shortstop as he covers the base.

Here is a play used at Lipscomb with runners on first and second base, no outs, and a close score in a late inning, when the defensive team cannot allow the offense to move a runner to third. The first and the third basemen play in. The shortstop and the second baseman play close to the base at second. The play should be called by you, the coach, and all infielders must know when it is to be executed. As the pitcher comes to his set position, he is looking toward second base. When he turns his head toward home plate, the shortstop sprints to third base, and the second baseman breaks for second. The pitcher turns his head back toward second, and if the runner has moved off the base, he turns and throws to it. If the second baseman's movement toward the base has caused the runner to shorten his lead, the pitcher throws the batter a waist-high fastball, directly over the middle of the plate. On the delivery to the batter, the first baseman and the third baseman charge as fast as they can and still maintain body balance. The player fielding the ball will throw to the shortstop covering third base (Diag. 13-25). It is important for the third baseman to wait for the pitcher's delivery before he charges toward the plate. Some base runners will try to outrun the shortstop to third base. If this happens, the pitcher can back off the rubber and throw to the third baseman, who can retreat several yards to cover the base.

When the squeeze play has been detected, the pitcher should throw a fastball inside and at the hips of a right-handed batter. This is a very difficult pitch to bunt. It is the job of the pitcher to throw an unbuntable pitch but one the catcher can handle. If the catcher is sure the squeeze play is on, he may call for a pitchout. If the batter is left-handed, the pitcher should throw outside, so he will have to step over home plate to reach it. Then the batter should be called out, and the runner returned to third base.

The catcher and the pitcher should remember that regardless of the pitch which may have been called, when the squeeze play breaks, it automatically is changed to a fastball.

The pitcher is the key player in breaking up the squeeze. The pitch delivered to the batter will determine to a large degree if the play succeeds or fails. The third baseman can help by alerting the pitcher when the runner leaves, and the catcher can help by reacting to the situation, but the only person who can break up the play is the pitcher.

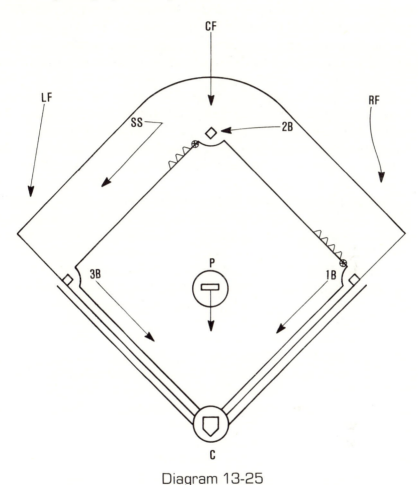

Diagram 13-25

DEFENSIVE STEAL SITUATIONS

SINGLE STEAL

When a runner is on first base, the catcher must be alert at all times for a possible steal. In a steal situation, he may call for a pitchout and try to pick off the runner at first or throw him out at second. If the runner should break from first base before the pitcher begins his delivery, he should step backward off the rubber and throw to the player covering second. The first baseman should be ready at all times to take a pickoff throw from either the pitcher or the catcher, while the player designated to cover second base must constantly watch the runner and be ready to receive a throw from the catcher.

With a runner on second base, the catcher should anticipate an attempted steal of third. In this situation, he may throw the runner out at third or trap him off second on a pitchout. If he breaks toward third base, the pitcher should quickly step back off the rubber and throw to the third baseman covering.

DOUBLE STEAL

In most cases, the batter determines whether the shortstop or the second baseman will cover on a double steal with first and third bases occupied. Usually it is the second baseman, because the majority of players are righthanded and hit to left field. The second baseman is the logical player to cover, since his approach to the base enables him to watch the runner on third. If the second baseman does not have a strong arm, it is preferable for the shortstop to take the throw. When covering the base in this situation, the infielder should make an attempt to reach the front of it, since this is the best position from which to run in on the ball should the runner on third start for the plate. If the runner on third shows no intentions of leaving that base, an attempt is made to tag the runner coming from first. If the runner approaching second base stops, the infielders start a rundown, while watching the runner on third, since most players attempt to break for the plate during the process of the rundown.

Some coaches prefer to defense the first and third situation by having one player cover and the other player stand 15 or 20 feet in front of the base in line with the throw. This permits the player in the short position to intercept the throw if the runner on third base attempts to score, or allows the throw to go through to the player covering second, should the runner remain at third. This method of covering the play requires either the shortstop or the second baseman to play out of position in order to reach this station in time for the throw, unless all batters are played to hit straightaway. However, this position may be necessary if neither the shortstop nor the second baseman has the arm to make the play from the base.

A clever catcher who "looks" the runner back at third, and infielders with strong arms will almost always prevent the offensive team from scoring under these circumstances. If the defensive team holds a commanding lead, the runner at third is disregarded. The game situation will always determine the strategy used concerning the runner at third. If he is the winning run, the fake to third is made, and the catcher throws back to the pitcher.

DELAYED STEAL

Occasionally a team will attempt a delayed steal. The runner on first may go all the way to second or stop halfway, with the intention of letting himself be trapped, so the man on third can score. The player who has the responsibility of covering second base should move several steps toward second after the ball has passed the batter, thus insuring that it will be covered if the runner does go all the way. When the runner leaves first, the first baseman should move down the line with him, so that in case he does stop halfway, the infielder covering at second can quickly relay the ball to the first baseman, who makes the tag and runs the ball in, to prevent the runner on third from scoring.

THE INTENTIONAL PASS

An intentional pass frequently is used as defensive strategy late in the game with second base or second and third base occupied and fewer than two outs. If the batter is the tying or winning run, it is not sound strategy to pass him intentionally.

Some coaches who have a left-handed pitcher on the mound will intentionally pass a right-handed batter to pitch to a left-handed hitter, if runners are in scoring position and first base is open. The intentional pass may be employed after a batter hits a double with the score tied and none out in the late innings. This creates a force-play situation at third base if the batter bunts, and a double-play situation if he hits away. If the first batter hits a triple in the last half of the last inning, the coach may issue two passes so that a force play is possible at the plate.

Usually, you will have the responsibility of deciding when an intentional pass will be issued. You may give this information by pointing to first base or using some vocal signal.

14

THE COACHING CHALLENGE

Coaching is one of the most challenging professions. It is very demanding, with many rewards coupled with headaches and heartaches.

The baseball coach is in a position that carries a great deal of responsibility; he has a unique opportunity to contribute to the development and education of young people. In performing his duties, he is constantly teaching.

The successful baseball coach will be a successful teacher. Teaching is an art that may be acquired and improved upon with practice. The personal philosophy of the coach will dictate the emphasis placed upon coaching. This philosophy is the way in which he views activities, events, and relationships, with the values he sets upon them. Too many people think the chief goal of a coach is to win more games than he loses. Therefore, they interpret his total philosophical makeup according to his attitude toward winning or losing. A more accurate analysis of his philosophy would be gained from knowing how he feels toward every facet of his job.

In order to better understand a coach's philosophy, one might observe the conduct of his players. Their style of play, the condition of their uniforms, the respect shown officials and opponents, the language used, their stamina in the late innings, their conduct off the field, their ability to withstand game pressure, their scholastic standing in the school, and the attitude of the student body and faculty toward them are just a few of the indicators of a coach's philosophy. They will show whether or not the coach considers the development of character traits to be important.

Baseball coaches create an image through their own personal appearance, language, behavior, and conduct. Teaching in this manner is more important to a coach than to any other member of the faculty, simply because of the difference between many of the objectives of an athletic program and those of other subject matter. Since baseball coaches are concerned with teaching attitudes and behavior among other things, these lessons can best be demonstrated by personal example.

In successfully teaching the fundamentals of baseball, the coach must understand two important factors: knowing how to recognize a mistake, and knowing how to correct it. This is the area where many baseball coaches fail to achieve success. When the coach recognizes a mistake, he must have the knowledge of the correct way in which an action should be performed or a play executed. Knowing how to correct a mistake is as important as being able to detect it. There is a rule used in all teaching which applies to baseball coaches—the student is responsible only for those things that he has been taught thoroughly. Successful coaches are constantly learning.

ORGANIZER

A good coach is a skillful teacher; a great coach is a superior teacher and organizer. The importance of sound organization is pointed out in the above statement and should never be underestimated.

Not all problems facing a coach are found on the playing field. The daily workout plan, the creation of a schedule, the purchase of equipment, and the preparation for games are a few examples. All of these are important aspects of coaching and require thoughtful consideration and careful planning.

An efficient baseball coach is constantly searching for materials and methods which not only will make his job a little easier but also will insure his doing a more thorough job of coaching. He may purchase additional equipment or hire several assistants. No single element guarantees success. Winning coaches have operated with no assistants, small squads, and a minimum of equipment. Conversely, losing teams have come from institutions which are blessed with the needed resources. How well the coach organizes the elements at his command largely will determine the success of his program.

FACULTY MEMBERS

One of the most powerful forces in the building of coaching character is affection. The most common form of its manifestation is gratitude. Showing affection makes the coach compassionate and understanding toward all persons. The expression of gratitude results in the faculty becoming involved in the problems of the coach. He must cultivate this spirit of affection for his fellow faculty members, and they will repay his efforts.

If a coach ascends the ladder of success, rest assured that a cooperative faculty has helped his climb. A coach's benefactors are the faculty. He must never alienate their interest. A hostile faculty can destroy the most successful coach. If the teachers respect the coach, they will give him the courage to accept defeat. They will be the professional mourners. Their kindness and understanding will give him the strength and courage to report to practice the next day.

One of the criticisms frequently leveled at coaches is that they often live in their own world with little regard for anything or anyone else and with little concern for the school as a whole. In some situations, no doubt, this is a legitimate criticism, while in others it may be unjustified. When coaches become so involved in baseball that they make little or no effort to show interest in other facets of the school, the assumption is that they just do not care.

A coach should not allow himself to be identified with this kind of image. It is important that the faculty realizes that the coach is concerned about something in addition to sports. His attendance at other school functions will impress faculty and students who are participating. This will allow everyone to observe him in a light other than that of the locker room or baseball field.

WINNING ATTITUDE

Proper attitude among the players is a must, if a coach expects to have a successful season. Their attitudes toward each other, the coaches, and all work are most important. Some players are not willing to pay the price demanded for a champion, and this weakness is the difference between their being fair and good or great and superior. They are not willing to come early and stay late or to run that extra lap when it hurts. Some players never know what they can do, because they never push themselves. To be a winner takes a proper frame of mind. Winning teams perpetuate worthy attitudes which stem from establishing winning habits.

Proper player attitudes will manifest themselves in a willingness to practice hard every day to perfect game skills. Players must possess a burning desire to improve if they have the winning outlook.

Pride must be mentioned as a significant element in attitude. Players must take pride in their play. They must hurt when they lose. Any player who loses and is satisfied does not have the winning spirit that all coaches are looking for.

TEAM MORALE

Morale is a mental state which renders a player capable of endurance and exhibiting courage in the presence of extreme difficulties. It may be defined further as a person's approach to problems concerned with self-assurance and persistence. Morale is a personal factor, but it also involves an identification of self with some group purpose. For identifying morale in an individual, the term most often used is courage, but in the group, it is spirit. Courage is the carrying out of a course of action in spite of extreme obstacles. Endurance refers to physical and mental lasting powers. It means resistance to fatigue and hurt when circumstances combine to make quitting easier than continuing the struggle.

It is the responsibility of the coach to develop a team morale which will give the group a feeling of oneness. To achieve this brand of morale, he must take many factors into consideration. First, he must make a close study of the personnel of his squad and learn each player's confidence by dealing fairly and honestly with all members of the team. Then, he must realize that the morale of the baseball team cannot be limited to the players and coaches. It involves the cooperation of the entire school. The administration and the faculty are very important in the development of this spirit.

The coach not only must sell the players on their own ability, but he also must sell the baseball program to the school and the community. The greatest factor in selling is enthusiasm. He must radiate that quality and develop it in each player.

TEAM DISCIPLINE

Discipline, the guidance and control of behavior, is a by-product of efficient coaching. It is a relationship, established by the coach, which draws from players the type of response that leads to successful performance on the field. No squad can live together in close proximity during the season without rules. Discipline cannot lose out to self-expression.

The observation of training rules is a must for team morale and discipline. If a member of the team disregards the rules and is not punished when caught, the morale of the team and respect for the coach decrease. Serious disciplinary problems should be handled in private. This immediately places the coach in the position of being a dictator, law maker, accuser, prosecutor, and judge. There is no higher appeal. However, he should never abuse this power, or he will lose a player's respect.

Discipline on the field will manifest itself in self-control later in life. This transfer is made possible because the moment a player yields to his impulses he gives up his right to play. Self-control requires courage. There is nothing more disconcerting than a player who is not his own master. During a close game when the going is tough and players are prone to anger, only the well-disciplined will obey the rules. Good discipline practiced every day enables players to keep a grip upon themselves regardless of pressure.

The moment a player receives his uniform, he becomes a member of a select group. He can take pride in being a part of something special. With this privilege, he must realize, belongs the responsibility for his conduct and appearance on and off the field. He must look and act like a gentleman, worthy of representing his school and its team.

PUBLIC RELATIONS

Public relations may be defined as the attitude of the public toward the baseball program. Pride in the profession is the first requisite for the coach to be effective in public relations. To be an outstanding public relationist, he must believe wholeheartedly in his vocation and in its importance to the entire educational system. Since the coach is in the public eye, he has a great opportunity to fulfill this role. If he is interested in all phases of the school, he can promote good relations not only for the baseball program but for other aspects of the school as well.

Effective public relations call for more than cordial contacts with the news media. The coach is being a public relationist when he takes time to participate in functions which are not school-related. He will be in demand as a speaker at civic organizations, church groups, alumni chapters, sport banquets, youth groups, and many other gatherings. Coaches should be articulate enough to present themselves in an interesting and sincere fashion.

If the coach is blessed with a sense of humor and the ability to speak, he will be a tremendous success. It is usually wise to "sense" the tone of the audience to determine on which aspects of his coaching to dwell during the speech. One pitfall to be avoided is the use of off-color stories or language. To resort to such tactics indicates a limited repertoire and degrades the profession.

The coach must be aware of the value of public relations. A sports program rarely can succeed without support from interested spectators and news media. The better informed the spectators, the more appreciative they are of the efforts of coaches and players. Proper public relations creates goodwill, sympathetic understanding, and active interest in the sports program.

DIPLOMAT

In spite of provocation, a coach should make every effort to avoid antagonizing people, particularly the parents of players. A clever "diplomat" learns how to react very quickly. When a straightforward, honest answer might be embarrassing to anyone concerned, especially parents, the coach will find himself playing this role.

This role is important in dealing with critics in the community. If such critics go unchecked, they may grow like a cancer and create serious problems for a coach. He, as a "diplomat," can do much toward preventing this kind of situation from getting out of hand or from being forced into a confrontation.

The "diplomat" knows that the time to make friends and firmly establish himself is when the team is winning and at the top. If the tide turns, the coach and his program will need every friend they can find. If they did not win allies when the team was riding the crest, they will not make them when they are losing.

ACTOR

Sometimes certain situations in coaching necessitate an acting role foreign to the coach's personality, such as scolding an individual or team when he prefers to remain calm, or "exploding" when it is best for the team to remain calm. On many occasions the coach will not be able to show his real emotions, like a broken heart when the team has lost the big game. The coach must ask himself what the right emotion is for the occasion. The pitfall to be avoided is that of being "phony." This would destroy what he is trying to do, since most young men are not deceived very long by insincerity. But, if the coach believes in what he is doing and recognizes that the situation calls for him to play this role in a certain way, he will find pretense to be an effective tool in accomplishing whatever the particular goal is at that moment.

The professional coach seldom fails to recognize these situations. However, they cannot always be anticipated, but with experience and common sense a teacher will be able to make a quick judgment as to the proper response. Always remember, teaching must be done when the situation is right, not when the player is discouraged, depressed, or angry.

INDEX